Horary Astrology
and the
Judgment of Events

Barbara H. Watters

Copyright 2012 by American Federations of Astrologers, Inc.
All rights reserved.

No part of this book may be reproduced or transcribed in any form or by any means, electronic or mechanical, including photocopying or recording or by any information storage and retrieval system without written permission from the author and publisher, except in the case of brief quotations embodied in critical reviews and articles. Requests and inquiries may be mailed to: American Federation of Astrologers, Inc., 6535 S. Rural Road, Tempe, AZ 85283.

ISBN-10: 0-86690-625-8
ISBN-13: 978-0-86690-625-8

Cover Design: Jack Cipolla

Published by:
American Federation of Astrologers, Inc.
6535 S. Rural Road
Tempe, AZ 85283

www.astrologers.com

Printed in the United States of America

Dedication

To my Students, whose

Diligence and Dedication made this book possible

Acknowledgments

I am most grateful to the following people for their help in preparing this book:

Timothy Murphy, for his research into the *Titanic* disaster; Svetlana Godillo, for the data used in chapter eight; Martha Taub, for her help; Barbara Kinsman, for her help; George Surmick, who provided me with transcripts of many of the tapes made in the classes where this work was developed; and all those who consented to allow the work done on their personal problems to be used in this book.

Contents

Part One

Chapter 1, What Horary Astrology Is	1
Chapter 2, How Horary Astrology Developed	7
Chapter 3, Strictures Against Judgment	11
Chapter 4, Signs and Rulers	15
Chapter 5, The Old Planets	31
Chapter 6, The New Planets	43
Chapter 7, The Houses	51
Chapter 8, Turning the Radical Chart	55
Chapter 9, Timing Events in the Horary Chart	63
Chapter 10, Placing Events in the Horary Chart	67
Chapter 11, The Aspects	71
Chapter 12, Further Considerations that Affect Judgment	75

Part Two

Chapter 13, Real Estate	91
Chapter 14, Employment	97
Chapter 15, Travel	103
Chapter 16, Multiple Questions	113
Chapter 17, Business, Finance, Investments	117
Chapter 18, Missing People	125
Chapter 19, Health	129
Chapter 20, Legal Problems	137
Chapter 21, Politics	155
Chapter 22, War	159

Part One

2/Horary Astrology and the Judgment of Events

1

What Horary Astrology Is

Horary astrology is the art of answering questions by analyzing a chart drawn for the moment the question is asked. The system of analysis is rigid. The rules are specific and easy to remember. The analysis is strictly confined to *the limits set by the question.*

Horary astrology is ancient. There seems little doubt that the traditions now associated with the analysis of the natal chart grew out of it. Astrology was first used to predict the fate of kings and nations. We now call this branch *mundane.*

Actually, mundane astrology has always used horary techniques with the focus of the questions shifted from the individual to a celestial event over which no individual has any control. From time immemorial the celestial events selected for mundane analysis have been lunations, eclipses, ingress charts for the equinoxes and solstices, the conjunctions of Jupiter and Saturn, the appearance of comets, and the movement of certain fixed stars in relation to the zodiacal point 0 Aries. While these mundane charts have always been cast for the occurrence of an uncontrollable celestial event, the purpose behind them was to answer questions that deeply concerned all the people of the nation: "Will we win the war?" "Will the crops be good?" "Will our herds increase?" "Will the barbarians attack us?" "Will the king live or die?"

The methods used to find answers to these questions were essentially horary methods. They were merely transferred to a larger frame of reference. If an individual asks, "Will my father recover from his illness?" the focus of the analysis centers around the same factors as when the nation is asking, "Will the king regain his health?" The fact that the individual asks the question consciously, aloud, while the concern of the nation may be unconscious and unspoken has nothing to do with the case. The astrologer uses the same significators and the same rigid horary conventions to answer either question. In fact, success in answering the question will largely depend upon forecasting in the most objective and impersonal manner possible. An honest question will elicit an honest answer from a chart that is correctly cast, *whether or not we like the answer.*

And there's the rub. The downfall of most horary and mundane work is wishful thinking. When a man asks, "Will my new business venture succeed?" the psychological impetus behind the question is an intense desire that it should succeed and fear that it won't. In subtle ways, the client communicates these emotions to the astrologer, who may then be reluctant to convey that there are indications the client will go bankrupt. The astrologer may begin to look for ways to soften the blow, which means searching the chart for ways out of impending bankruptcy. The intense concentration applied to the search for a way out results in *changing the question* in the astrologer's mind, while being unaware that this has happened.

The question was "Will my business venture succeed?" to which the answer was a clear "No." The question in the astrologer's mind becomes, "How can this man avoid bankruptcy?" Since the client desperately wants a favorable answer, and the astrologer has subtly changed the meaning of the question (quite unconsciously and with the best intentions), neither will notice that the answer applies to a hypothetical question *which was never asked.* During this process, the factors pertinent to the real question, which should have been kept rigidly in the foreground of consciousness, slide into the background where they can be comfortably ignored-until the man goes bankrupt, of course.

If, instead of going to an astrologer, the client had gone to a bookkeeper, and the bookkeeper had told him that he could get out of debt by assuming that two and two equal five, the client would think the bookkeeper had lost his mind. When the astrologer or the client changes the focus of the question, both of them, inspired by wishful thinking, they have subconsciously accepted the proposition that two and two make five. The result of this well-meaning deceit brings to light another precept of horary astrology: a dishonest question yields a dishonest answer. That is, a *false* answer.

The first inviolate rule of horary astrology is: State the question as clearly and explicitly as possible. Write it down with the exact time of asking. Keep this always before you. And *never change the question by a single word.* The horary chart applies *only* to the question asked at that moment. It will yield no answer whatever to a question that was not asked. And it will yield no information on collateral matters that have nothing to do with the case, even though these matters may be of equal concern at the same time.

The only way around this is to ask another question, such as, "Is there anything I can do to avoid bankruptcy or prevent it?" A follow-up question like this makes the tacit assumption that bankruptcy will result from allowing things to continue as they are. By acting to change the status quo, events may be channeled into another course that is more favorable to the querent. Since the second question will always be asked at a later time, it will yield a different chart, which means a new perspective. But it must be a *different question,* however closely related to the first one.

The second inviolate rule of horary astrology is: Never ask the same question twice in the same set of circumstances hoping to get a different answer. The chart cast for the first time the question is asked produces the only valid answer. All attempts to change this by making multiple charts for different times result only in confusion and dishonesty.

In horary astrology there are four conditions called "strictures against judgment." If a chart is cast for a time when anyone of these conditions prevails, it cannot be read. This often inspires the client or student to ask the same question again at a later time or on a different day, hoping for better luck. One of the strangest things about horary astrology is that no matter how often this question is asked, the result will a chart with a stricture against judgment or one which, for some other reason, will not yield an answer. This is a clear warning against the practice of repeatedly asking the same question, and it comes from within the horary discipline itself. Just as disobeying the laws of arithmetic will never balance the bankrupt's books, so disobeying the laws of horary astrology will never produce a useful answer to any question.

This is probably one reason why horary astrology began to fall into disrepute toward the end of the nineteenth century. Its rigid rules, its strictures against judgment, its dogmatic Yes-No answers, all smacked of fortune-telling and fatalism. Beginning with Alan Leo and the Theosophists, the ancient pragmatic basis of astrology slowly shifted to something very like a religious psychological basis. The nineteenth century belief in progress and the optimism that resulted from what appeared to be man's scientific mastery over Nature made even astrologers feel that they were masters of their fates and captains of their souls. In the myths of the time, virtue always triumphed, every Cinderella married a prince, every seventh son became a millionaire, everyone could succeed if he worked hard enough, and the poor who are always with us had only themselves to blame. It was not merely socially unacceptable to question any of these myths, it was downright blasphemous.

The temper of the times was one of sanctimonious arrogance. Like everyone else, astrologers are educated in their times, molded by the laws and customs of their society, and brought up to believe in the prevailing social philosophy. Unfortunately, the whole concept of astrology in all its branches is antipathetic to scientific materialism, to the Victorian notion that Man is somehow immune to natural laws, and that the Universe is a vast machine that Man can manipulate for his own advantage. Astrology cannot accept this basic philosophy for a very simple reason: if it does, it cannot function, it will not work. When a body of knowledge cannot be made to work within the frame of the prevailing social philosophy, it falls into disrepute. It is classified by the learned, who are those who function best in the frame of the social philosophy, as a "superstition." All respectable intellectuals ignore it, all religions condemn it. The few hardy spirits who continue to practice it are regarded with suspicion and treated with mockery.

This is what happened to astrology in the nineteenth century. Interest in it could be revived only if the basic social philosophy changed, or if some person, like Alan Leo, deliberately and consciously restated the principles of astrology in such a way as to minimize the contradictions between the two systems. For astrology to survive and function in the age of scientific arrogance, it was necessary to find some part of the ancient knowledge that agreed with some aspect of the prevailing materialistic social philosophy. Alan Leo found this common meeting ground in the concept of free will. Natal astrology was the branch where free will could be constantly emphasized without doing too much violence to the basic astrological law: "As above, so below."

By constant emphasis upon free will, Alan Leo's followers gradually built up a system of natal astrology which implied that, regardless of your natal chart, you were free to choose to do and be anything you wanted, provided that you responded to the "higher vibrations." The horoscope came to be regarded as a psychological mirror in which the inner nature of the man was reflected. "Bad" aspects gradually became "difficult," then "challenging." Malefics gradually became "disciplinary influences." What mattered was not the aspects and the planets themselves, but how they were used.

There is much to be said for this viewpoint of the natal chart. Most of us today practice this type of natal astrology. It works fairly well in a society where education is universal and many different kinds of opportunity are open to each person. It would fail to work in a slave society, in an absolute tyranny, or in a society in the grip of a terrible disaster. It may work to save your life if you can get an operation in time. But it will not work to save your life if an atomic bomb falls suddenly on your city. In other words, the modern concept of the natal chart that you are free to develop every position and aspect of your horoscope constructively; or that you can choose the way you will go, can be maintained only by people who live in a relatively free society.

When this view of the natal chart is transferred to either horary or mundane astrology, it becomes wishful thinking. An individual may learn to use Mars square Saturn constructively, but no amount of free choice or desire will transform this into a good aspect in a horary chart. Anyone who tries to do so will get a false answer. If you get enough false answers, you stop asking questions. For this reason horary astrology is still in disrepute among us.

Remember that few people really want to know the truth. They are content to be told that what they already believe is true.

2

How Horary Astrology Developed

Horary astrology and its related field, mundane, did not develop in free societies. They developed in societies where the majority of people were slaves and where all people, even kings and high priests, were constantly aware of human bondage to Nature. Surrounded by desert, Egypt was a narrow green ribbon wholly dependent upon the annual Nile flood. Mesopotamia was a barren plain cut by two rivers that tended to dry up in the summer; water was, therefore, hoarded in reservoirs and rationed to the fields through an elaborate system of irrigation ditches. Trade was as precarious as agriculture, for it meant that people had to travel thousands of miles through hostile country, across deserts and mountains; or, like the Greeks and Phoenicians, take to the dangerous sea in frail ships. Who knew, when setting out, if he would ever return?

Throughout its long history, Egypt suffered few invasions because the deserts on either side were too formidable for primitive armies to cross. But the Mesopotamian cities on the open plain were constantly harried by fierce nomadic tribes, jealous of their wealth. Like the Indians of the American West, bands of Bedouins would suddenly swoop down on lonely outposts, killing or enslaving everyone. Then who could say, when he went out in the morning to tend his flocks or his fields, that night would see him safely back inside the city walls?

Human existence was precarious. Every bowl of food, every drop of water, every shekel earned in trade, every day of life was snatched in peril from an unfriendly world. Each man lived in the constant awareness that his existence depended upon the sufferance of jealous gods. At any moment, and for no reason a man could understand, divine tolerance might suddenly cease, and he and *all his people* might be wiped out. Therefore, it behooved people to pay strict attention to everything that went on in this cruel, inscrutable world that held the power of life and death. Never for a moment could it be forgotten that Nature was more powerful than any human, whether a king or a slave, and everyone was in bondage to it.

Nothing was more real than the capricious power of the external world. And Man had a name for that capricious power; it was called Fate. People lived from day to day with one consuming desire: to get the best of it for another twenty-four hours. I think it probable that the whole development of human culture and the evolution of the human brain has been a response to the human desire to be free from the bondage of Fate.

Aeschylus wrote: Zeus alone is free. His word for freedom was *autarkia,* which meant "absolute power to do what one wished and to command anything one wanted." In English we call this autocracy, which to us means absolute tyranny.

People who believe that Nature, society, and other people have no influence on their lives and no power over them should stay away from horary astrology. They are like Zeus, secure in their *autarkia.* This branch of our art, the only one that still consciously struggles to outwit Fate, has nothing to offer them.

Einstein said, "Physics assumes the existence of an external world." So does horary astrology. It also assumes, along with historians and sociologists, the existence of a social world. And, following the dictates of experience and common sense, it further assumes the existence of other people we know—our family, friends, and associates. Every valid horary question will concern a *limited* relationship between the querent and one or more of these outer worlds, which are objective to him and which he does not absolutely control. If such a relationship exists, the chart will reveal whether it is favorable or unfavorable. If there is no valid relationship (although the querent may think there is), a stricture against judgment will appear in the chart, which means it cannot yield an answer.

If the querent asks about an external situation so vast and powerful in relation to himself that nothing he does can affect it or change it, the answer will be false or ambiguous. For example, there will be no reliable answer to a question about when a war will be over, because, in relation to the war, the querent is powerless. Nothing he does can circumvent the destiny of the war. But if someone wants to know when their son will return from the war, a straight answer will be given because the relationship between a parent and their child is both viable and limited.

If the querent asks about an inner problem unrelated to anything in the external world, there will not be an answer either. For instance, there will not be an answer to the question: "Will I ever be cured of my neurosis?" This is because neurosis is an emotional maladjustment within someone's own psyche, and the "war" is within that person. While the neurosis may be projected upon the external world, it has no real existence apart from the querent. But if someone asks whether or not their spouse will ever be cured of a neurosis, a valid answer can be found, because there is a valid, limited relationship with another person about whom the querent is deeply concerned.

In using the horary technique, always bear these distinctions in mind. Refrain from asking about things that are none of your business.

There is one more limitation of horary astrology that must never be forgotten. No matter how alarming a horary chart may be, it never reveals the death of the querent nor anything about the circumstances of his death. Horary charts frequently reveal the death of other people who have or had valid relationships with the querent, but never *the querent's* death. The reason is obvious: death solves all problems, ends all conflicts, and puts a stop to all viable, limited relations with the external world of material affairs for that individual. Questions can only apply to relations within this world and its special, limited circumstances. Death moves us into another, unknown world about which horary astrology has nothing whatever to say.

3

Strictures Against Judgment

If any of the following conditions occur in a chart set up to answer a question, we say that the chart is not radical and it cannot be judged.

1. Void-of-course Moon. The Moon is void of course when it makes no major aspect to another planet before it leaves the sign it is in. The major aspects are: conjunction, trine, square, sextile, opposition, quincunx, parallel, and contraparallel. Some people include the semisextile, semisquare, and sesquiquadrate, but I have not found them effective in preventing the dead-end result that comes from a void-of-course Moon condition.

Example: I am writing this on February 24, 1972. The Moon is in Cancer. At 9:01 p.m. EST it makes a square aspect to Uranus in Libra. From that moment until February 25, at 7:17 p.m. EST, when it enters Leo, it makes no aspect to another planet. Therefore, any chart cast to answer a question from 9:01 p.m. on the 24th to 7:17 p.m. on the 25th will find this stricture against judgment present. According to the rules of horary astrology, such a chart will not be radical and cannot be read.

The reason for this stricture is that, in horary astrology, the Moon rules *function*. When it makes no aspect to another planet until after it leaves the sign it is in, nothing functions in the situation that gave rise to the question. Therefore, until circumstances change, which they will do when the Moon moves into the next sign, the situation is not viable. The question has no future as things stand. This may be because the question was unnecessary or of no real concern to the querent. It may also be because vital facts pertaining to the problem are unknown to him. Most commonly it means that in the very near future something unforeseen will happen that will render the whole matter of the question null and void.

For instance, suppose the querent asks if he will get a certain job. A void-of-course Moon in the chart often means that it makes no difference whether or not he gets it because in the near future, perhaps even in a day or so, he won't want it or can't accept it. He may be offered a better job, he may suddenly have to move, or circumstances surrounding the job he asked about may change so radically that it becomes undesirable. But whatever the reason, do not try to find it in a void-of-course Moon chart. You can't. The chart is inscrutable because the question was asked about a dead-end issue.

2. Saturn in the seventh house. In the horary chart, the first house rules the querent and the seventh rules the astrologer. Saturn falling there indicates that the astrologer's judgment is clouded. Frequently, an error has been made in casting the chart, or the astrologer may have misunderstood the question or written it down wrong. The reason for this blindness hardly matters because if judgment is clouded the astrologer cannot be objective, and without objectivity the client is not served well. If you are your own astrologer casting a chart for yourself, Saturn in the first may have the same effect.

3. The Moon in the Via Combusta. The ancients called the section of the zodiac from 15 Libra to 15 Scorpio the Via Combusta, which means "the Fiery Road." This 30-degree section was regarded as the most dangerous in the zodiac, probably because two to three thousand years ago it coincided with the constellation Scorpio, which contains many dangerous fixed stars. Some of these, like Antares and the North Scale, have now moved on into early Sagittarius or late Scorpio, and the two great benefic stars of Libra, Spica and Arcturus, have moved up to 23 and 24 Libra. Nevertheless, the stricture still stands, although it is hard to see why it should.

For several years I tried to ignore it when reading horary charts. I found that the effect of the Moon in the Via Combusta was much like a conjunction of the Moon with Uranus. Events took a sudden, unpredictable turn that contradicted the reading and was not advantageous to the querent. Usually the event was connected with violence, a social or natural disaster, war, or accidents. Sometimes it was the sudden death of a person on whom the outcome depended, or the destruction of the property asked about. Needless to say, I went back to observing the stricture.

4. Less than 3 degrees or more than 27 degrees of a sign rising. In the first case, the matter asked about is not ripe enough to yield a solution to the question, or the question is premature. In the second case, the matter asked about has already been settled or is so close to a conclusion that the question is irrelevant.

This is the only stricture against judgment to which there is an exception, and it is this: if the degree and minute rising is in exact conjunction with a natal planet in the querent's chart, the question asked is considered to be one of special importance. The natal planet which is exactly rising in the horary chart is then incorporated into it and is taken as the horary ruler and everything else is read in relation to it. The result may be extremely illuminating.

To take advantage of this exception you must have the querent's correct natal chart, as no orbs greater than 10 minutes of arc can be allowed. Only the conjunction permits this exception. You cannot say you'll go ahead and read the chart because the horary Ascendant is exactly trine your Venus. Only a natal planet can be used; a midpoint will not validate the horary chart.

If the planet making the conjunction is a benefic or the significator of the question, the chances of a favorable outcome are increased. For instance, the querent who makes her living as a model asks, "Shall I have my face lifted? I'm getting on and losing jobs because of it." If her natal Venus is exactly rising in the horary chart, the answer would probably be yes unless there were many serious afflictions from the horary malefics.

A neutral planet rising, or the natal Mars, usually means that the querent will have to do whatever has been asked about, because he will have no choice in the matter, especially if the rising natal planet is a significator in the question. Suppose the client asks if he should sign certain legal papers, and his natal Mercury, the significator of signing papers, is exactly rising. He is in a forced situation where he *has* to sign, but unless the Mercury is seriously afflicted, it will probably be to his advantage.

If the querent's natal Saturn is exactly rising, the question asked is not the one on the his mind. He is really troubled about something that is a very grave matter, but he is afraid to ask. He is in some sort of bind he cannot discuss, and he sees no way out. He asks a question about something else in the hope the answer will provide a solution to his unspoken problem. For instance, the natal Saturn may be rising on an invalid horary Ascendant of a querent who is contemplating suicide, of one who has committed a crime, of one who suspects he has a fatal disease but is afraid to go to a doctor, or of one whose whole life is based on a lie, like a bigamist, a secret agent, or someone traveling on forged papers.

When the natal Saturn rises on the invalid Ascendant, even if well aspected and a significator of the question asked, the querent should be warned against doing what he asks about. Suppose he asks about the wisdom of buying a certain house. Saturn is the significator of real estate, and it is well aspected. He should be advised not to buy because *he does not really want the house.* Or the underlying situation that troubles him is so grave he will never have any use for the house.

Never ask such a querent what he really fears. What the client refuses to talk about is not your business: it is not part of the astrologer's function to pry. If you must know the true state of affairs, study the natal chart. But do not reveal what you discover to anyone else.

14/Horary Astrology and the Judgment of Events

4

Signs and Rulers

Horary astrology is concerned with circumstances, usually of a limited and transitory nature. Therefore, the signs of the zodiac, which describe innate temperament and character, are of less importance than the houses, which describe what we do with our innate qualities, how we function in the accidental circumstances of our :lives, and our relations with others.

This is the opposite of natal astrology, where the signs are more important than the houses. Natal astrology makes the assumption that character is fate. From this it follows that by changing our character, we can change our fate, which in turn will change our reaction to circumstances and to other people. Natal astrology operates in a framework of *cycles,* which describe life as a process of growth, change, and decay. These cycles are measured along the ecliptic, which is the plane of the Earth's orbit around the Sun. Natal astrology is a Sun-oriented system.

Horary astrology makes the assumption that circumstance is fate. It operates in a framework of *events* which describe life as a series of incidents, a history, or drama. This series is measured by the daily spin of the Earth on its axis. Horary time is not a cycle. It is clock time, measured from one sunrise to the next, and is a Moon-oriented system.

The horary chart is a picture of an event frozen in time. Any development of this event is inherent in the moment of its initiation. If this were not the case, we could never predict the outcome of anything.

Such importance as the signs do retain is expressed through their most materialistic meanings, through their elements and qualities, through their planetary rulers, and through their governance of parts of the body. A great deal of the sign meaning in horary astrology is discovered through analogy with the position of the sign in the natural zodiac. This is equated with the circumstantial meaning of the houses. But also, as in natal astrology, the meaning of the sign is colored by the nature of the planet ruling it. Success in horary astrology depends upon paying close attention to this interlocking network of meanings. It is almost impossible to memorize all the meanings of every sign, house, and planet. Therefore, it becomes necessary to train yourself to think in analogies, so that one meaning suggests another, which in turn suggests still others. With practice, this process soon becomes automatic. Then wresting the meaning from a horary chart is fun, much like working a puzzle.

In many questions, the signs give useful clues about the appearance or occupation of a person, about disease, the kind and quality of land, places, and objects.

Aries

Ruler: Mars   *Quality*: Cardinal   *Element*: Fire

This first sign of the zodiac is masculine, positive, diurnal, changeable, fiery, hot, dry, choleric, bestial; impetuous, intemperate, violent, spendthrift, courageous, rebellious, outspoken, restless, active.

Its color is red.

It rules the head and the brain (as an organ of the body).

Among diseases, it signifies boils, acne, ringworm, smallpox, scarlet fever, epilepsy, cerebral hemorrhage, migraine, toothaches, cuts and wounds, excessive bleeding, ruptures, and hernia.

Among places, it signifies land that is barren, sandy, eroded, and sometimes hilly, or new land, recently settled and cleared for cultivation; dry pastures; deserts; stables for small animals; tents or temporary dwellings; hiding places for fugitives; and unfrequented or unexplored places.

Among things, it signifies the roof, ceiling, and plastering in houses; sheep; knives and other sharp instruments; weapons; furnaces and kilns; broken objects; iron and steel, or objects made of them; fires and burnt objects; strong spices, like pepper; the dawn of a new day, hence the early morning hours; blood or bloodstains.

Among people and occupations, it rules nomads; shepherds or sheep farmers; surgeons; soldiers; blacksmiths; explorers; hunters; the leader of a band, especially of criminals or rebels; one who has recently left or strayed from home; and pioneers.

Among countries, it is said to rule England, Germany, Denmark, Western Poland, Palestine, Syria, and Italy from Naples south.

Its direction is east.

It is the exaltation of the Sun and the detriment of Venus.

Taurus

Ruler: Venus   *Quality*: Fixed   *Element*: Earth

This second sign of the zodiac is feminine, negative, nocturnal, cold, dry, melancholy, bestial, patient, slow to change, stubborn, quiet, conservative, materialistic, clumsy, slow-spoken, comfort-loving, a creature of routine habits who sometimes bursts out in uncontrollable rages.

Its colors are brown and blue.

It rules the neck and throat.

Among diseases, it signifies sore throat; goiter; tonsillitis; accidents or wounds to the throat or neck; choking. In cases of extreme affliction, it may be a significator of hanging or beheading.

Among places, it signifies dairy barns; stables for horses; low houses in the country; cottages; fertile pastures; fields of grain; banks or counting houses; granaries; in houses, the basement and low rooms; land that is fertile, under cultivation, or sparsely wooded.

Among things, it signifies what is close to the ground or floor; cattle; dairy equipment; plows; purses, safes, safe deposit boxes; money or valuables belonging to the querent; bronze or objects made of it; objects placed under other things, like footstools or trundle beds; choirs and glee clubs; song birds; country fairs; bull rings.

Among people and occupations, it rules dairy farmers; cattle breeders; cowboys; stable hands; bankers and money lenders; architects; throat specialists; singers; sculptors; road builders; and insurance brokers.

Among countries, it is said to rule Ireland, Persia, eastern Poland, Asia Minor, Cyprus, and southern Russia.

Its direction is south by east.

It is the exaltation of the Moon and the detriment of Mars.

This sign is unfriendly to Pluto.

Gemini

Ruler: Mercury   *Quality*: Mutable   *Element*: Air

This sign is masculine, positive, diurnal, hot, moist, sanguine, human, double-bodied, nervous, quick to change, flighty, talkative, idealistic, clever, liberty-loving, inventive, curious, intellectual, emotionally shallow, childlike, nimble, light-fingered, fickle, and democratic.

Its colors are piebald and yellow.

It rules the hands, arms, shoulders, lungs, and respiration.

Among diseases, it signifies asthma, tuberculosis, emphysema, pneumonia, illnesses affecting the nerves, uncontrollable tics and tremors, accidents, wounds and crippling of the hands, arms, and shoulders. Severely afflicted, it may indicate mental illness, delusions, and hallucinations.

Among places, it signifies the halls of houses; game-rooms; elementary schools and nurseries; tennis courts; playgrounds; tool sheds; corn cribs; airy barns; hills and mountains; high places; land that is open, wind-swept, and well-drained; the suburbs.

Among things, it signifies the walls of houses; wainscoting and wallpaper; boxes for papers and knickknacks; desks; high chests; bookshelves; books; manuscripts; documents of all kinds; lists; newspapers and magazines; writing implements; letters; telephones and other small appliances used every day; short journeys; commuting; vehicles used in everyday transportation, such as cars, buses, bicycles; small birds; rumors; gossip; linens; playing cards; monkeys; games like chess and dominoes; small gadgets and labor-saving devices; watches, thermometers; measuring tools; the metal mercury.

Among people and occupations, it rules pickpockets, thieves, forgers, liars, messengers, neighbors, twins, reporters, writers; door-to-door salesmen; lecturers; elementary and high school teachers; inventors; mimics; mathematicians; scientists; comedians; merchants; and traders.

Among countries, it is said to rule the United States, Lower Egypt, northeastern Italy, Belgium, west of England, and London.

Its direction is west by south.

It is the exaltation of the Moon's North Node and the detriment of Jupiter.

Cancer

Ruler: Moon   *Quality*: Cardinal   *Element*: Water

This fourth sign of the zodiac is feminine, negative, nocturnal, cold, moist, fruitful, phlegmatic, mute, patient, conservative, practical, home-loving, sympathetic, emotional, maternal, faithful, long-suffering, stable, desirous of security, and sentimental.

Its colors are milk-white and green.

It rules the breast, stomach, and womb.

Among diseases, it signifies dropsy, stomach ulcers, menstrual disorders, malfunctioning of the stomach, diphtheria, poliomyelitis, and, in general, both the diseases of childhood and those which, in adult life, are caused by psychological or emotional problems. It is a sign addicted to hypochondria and the over-consumption of sweets. When badly afflicted, there may be cancer of the breast, stomach, or uterus. Ancient astrologers thought this disease took its name from the sign, but it seems more likely that it was named "crab" because of its crab-like spread in the final stages. An astrologer should never attempt to diagnose this or any other disease from a horary chart. The medical significators given in this book are for descriptive purposes only. No astrologer is qualified to practice medicine unless he is also a physician.

From the most ancient times, however, Cancer has been one of the signs associated with poor health, especially in childhood. Virgo, Capricorn, and Pisces are the others. The star Castor, now at 19 Cancer, is associated with crippling. Severely afflicted planets on this point frequently correlate with a malformation of the body, usually congenital or caused by disease; if there are many planets in Aries, or if Mars afflicts, it may be caused by accident.

Among places, Cancer signifies the sea, rivers, lakes, beaches, brooks, springs, marshes or ditches where reeds grow; bars, restaurants, the ship's hold, and laboratories. In general, it rules the home; and within houses underground cellars, laundry rooms, bathrooms, kitchens, cisterns; the vegetable garden. The kind of land it denotes is fertile, bordering on water or containing ponds, brooks, springs, and wells.

Among things it signifies amphibious creatures like crabs and frogs; water birds; boats; liquid stores of food, especially milk; caves; containers for food and liquids; eggs; nests; incubators; pumps; embryos; childbirth, newborn animals, pregnancy; the metal silver and objects made of it; ferns; rushes; grottoes; spas and healing waters; charitable organizations devoted to feeding people; nourishment in general.

Among people and occupations, it rules cooks; wet nurses; sailors; bartenders; small infants; pediatricians and gynecologists; laboratory technicians; organic chemists; nurserymen; housekeepers; gardeners; domestics, in general; real-estate developers and others who deal in houses; landlords; people who organize and dispense charity.

Among countries, it is said to rule the Netherlands, Scotland, Russian Georgia, and all of Africa. Among cities: Constantinople, Tunis, Algiers, Amsterdam, Venice, Genoa, Manchester in England, New York, Bern, and Milan.

Its direction is north.

It is the exaltation of Jupiter, the fall of Mars, and the detriment of Saturn.

Leo

Ruler: Sun   *Quality*: Fixed   *Element*: Fire

This fifth sign of the zodiac is hot, dry, choleric, diurnal, bestial, barren, masculine, positive, commanding, dogmatic, strong, active, valiant, courteous, imperial, proud, generous, lavish, outspoken, honest, lacking in malice, susceptible to flattery, creative, and optimistic.

Its colors are gold and orange.

It rules the heart, arteries, spine, upper back, and ribs.

Among diseases, it signifies coronary thrombosis; palpitations and other malfunctioning of the heart; wounds and accidents to the back and sides; dangerously high fevers, infections or injuries to the eyes. Blindness is associated with 6 Leo. Physically, Leo is the strongest sign of the zodiac. It has enormous powers of recuperation. Even when it appears frail, it has remarkable endurance. The principal danger to health and life comes from Leo's refusal to give in, to be ill, or to take care of itself. Leo dies with its boots on, usually without warning in the midst of work or play. Leos who live to a very advanced age usually pass away in their sleep.

In ancient times, Leo was thought to rule the plague, pestilence, and yellow jaundice. Now that we know what causes these diseases, we place the rulership under the signs that govern the causative factors rather than under the sign describing the symptoms. Two logical exceptions, however, would be cholera and yellow fever. The first is an intestinal disease, but its victims die of dehydration. The second, although caused by mosquitoes, produces killing fevers of the Leo type.

Among places, it signifies areas frequented by wild beasts; jungles; forests; veldts; inaccessible places like; steep cliffs, mountain tops or sides; rocky places; stony deserts; palaces, castles; forts; parks; arenas; theatres; zoos; wildlife preserves; hunting grounds; stages; houses of the "showplace" type, or those preserved as monuments to which the public is admitted for a fee; hotels; stock exchanges; and museums. In houses, it rules the hearth, fireplaces, chimneys, stoves, and ovens.

Among things it signifies wild beasts, particularly feral cats; honeybees; circuses; birds of gaudy plumage, like peacocks; sumptuous fabrics; crowns; precious jewelry; lamps; appliances that produce heat; theatrical trappings and costumes; hunting gear; toys; anything used to pursue a hobby; secondary schools; anything overly ostentatious; the metal gold and articles made of it; speculation; works of art; the drama; luxurious furs; among foods, meat, especially game.

Among people and occupations it signifies one's own children; young unmarried people; kings, queens, princes; lovers; hotel keepers; bee keepers; gypsies; actors; artists; dramatists; hobbyists; amateurs who pursue any art, craft, sport for love of it; the host at a party; goldsmiths; heart specialists; ambassadors; circus performers; hunters and trappers of large wild animals; people who live a carefree, bohemian existence; foresters; game wardens; fire fighters; boxers; theatrical producers or directors; owners of places of amusement, arenas, theatres; in a business, the treasurer; athletic coaches; stock brokers; speculators.

Among countries, it is said to rule France, Italy, Bohemia, and Sicily. Among cities: Rome, Prague, Philadelphia, and Chicago. It also rules the Alps. In ancient astrology, it ruled the Roman Empire, Chaldea, and Babylon.

Its direction is east by north.

No planet is exalted in Leo. It is the detriment of Saturn.

This sign is unfriendly to Uranus.

Virgo

Ruler: Mercury   *Quality*: Mutable   *Element*: Earth

This sixth sign of the zodiac is cold, barren, melancholy, feminine, negative, nocturnal, critical, efficient, retiring, human, studious, analytical, shrewish, inquisitive, busy, neat, fussy, somewhat niggardly, fastidious, old-maidish, conservative, and pessimistic.

Its color is violet.

It rules the intestines and the process of digestion.

Among the diseases, it signifies intestinal parasites, food allergies, diet deficiency diseases, constipation, diverticulitis, digestive disorders, obstructions of the intestines, gastroenteritis, and dysentery. Although Virgo is said to govern health, in general, because it is the sixth sign, it is not physically strong. Its mind is overly preoccupied with its body and with bodily processes that should be unconscious, automatic. A hypochondriac, fussy eater, or pill taker, a compulsive housekeeper, a food faddist, and fearful of germs and infections. Many Virgo ills arise from these tendencies, and they make themselves sick over constant concern with their health.

Among places, Virgo signifies study halls; libraries; bookkeeping offices; rooming houses; servants' quarters; granaries; grocery and drug stores; hay-ricks; silos; warehouses where food is stored; fields of grain or silage crops like alfalfa, clover, and hay. In houses, it signifies the study or den; closets; pantries; cupboards or shelves for food; and medicine chests. In real estate, it denotes two kinds of property: open arable fields, somewhat dry; and buildings of an unostentatious, utilitarian type that are rented to working-class tenants or people of modest means. Virgo property may be highly profitable, but it is dreary.

Among things, Virgo signifies ledgers and account books; foods; medicines; herbs; cotton, cotton textiles, and weaving and spinning equipment; sewing machines; diet regimens; spiders; pet animals, especially cats; pockets; the civil service; typewriters; computers; cookbooks; animal hospitals; mice; poultry; anything of a markedly utilitarian nature, or designed to be serviceable.

Among people and occupations, it signifies bookkeepers; accountants; secretaries; typists; textile workers; dressmakers; veterinarians; dieticians; homeopathic physicians; pharmacists; nurses; members of the armed forces; civil servants; tailors; servants, in general; one's tenants; printers; librarians; shop clerks; office workers; employees; spinsters; computer programmers; clock makers; people who tend or repair precision instruments; agents of all types, such as travel agents, booking agents, literary agents, or people delegated to act for you as agents.

Among countries, it is said to rule Turkey, Switzerland, Mesopotamia, and the West Indies. Among cities: Paris, Lyons, Toulouse, Heidelberg, Jerusalem, Baghdad, and Liverpool.

Its direction is south by west.

It is the exaltation of Mercury, the fall of Venus, and the detriment of Jupiter. This sign is unfriendly to Neptune.

Libra

Ruler: Venus   *Quality*: Cardinal   *Element*: Air

This seventh sign of the zodiac is hot, moist, sanguine, masculine, positive, equinoctial, moveable, diurnal, human, vacillating, compromising, peace loving, elegant, tasteful, lazy, charming, just, rational, tactful, forbearing, amiable, compliant, and vain.

Its colors are pastel hues and coral.

It rules the kidneys and lower back.

All diseases of the kidneys or accidents to them; weak back and backaches, which are frequently caused by poor posture. Many Librans are addicted to sweets and may become obese in middle age.

Among places, it signifies the open fields near windmills; straggling barns or outhouses like tobacco barns or woodsheds; saw mills; lumber yards; furniture factories; hunting grounds for birds, especially with hawks; hillsides; hilltops; gravel and sand pits; places where the air is especially clear and sharp; the open streets in cities; the forums or town squares; court houses; places where legal documents are registered and stored; fine art museums; beauty parlors; salons of dressmakers and interior decorators; jewelry stores; flower gardens. In houses: the upper rooms; bed chambers; attics; any room which is inside another; the tops of chests, wardrobes, and high cupboards. In real estate it describes wooded, hilly land, somewhat sandy; elegant city or town houses in good neighborhoods; luxury apartments or the buildings that contain them.

Among things, it rules strategy; peace; marriage; legal partnerships; treaties; allies; public enemies; wood and wooden objects; copper and copper objects; fashionable clothes; elegant fabrics; falcons and falconry; perfumes and cosmetics; valuable bibelots; upholstery; and lace.

Among people and occupations, it signifies generals; strategists; hairdressers; perfumers; cosmeticians; interior designers; upholsterers; cabinet makers and carpenters; foresters; criminal lawyers; divorce lawyers; dandies; clothes models; fashionable women; marriage counselors; coppersmiths; artists and those of artistic inclinations; art dealers; dress designers; and dance teachers.

Among countries, it is said to rule China, Japan, northern India, West Pakistan, Austria, Upper Egypt, and areas near the Caspian Sea. Among cities, it rules Lisbon, Vienna, Antwerp, Frankfort, and Charleston, South Carolina.

Its direction is west.

It is the exaltation of Saturn, the fall of the Sun, and the detriment of Mars.

Scorpio

Ruler: Mars (Pluto) *Quality*: Fixed *Element*: Water

This eighth sign of the zodiac is cold, nocturnal, feminine, negative, fruitful, phlegmatic, repressed, subtle, deceitful, secretive, magnetic, emotional, passionate, preoccupied with hidden things, devious, clever in solving puzzles, often of superior intelligence.

Its colors are maroon and purple.

It rules the bladder, vagina, testicles, the groin, the penis, the anus, and the process of elimination.

Among diseases, it signifies afflictions of the bladder; hernias in the groin; hemorrhoids; gonorrhea; syphilis; castration; hysterectomy; infections or plagues caused by vermin like typhus or bubonic plague; diseases caused by stinging insects; perils from surgery or torture.

Among places, it signifies sewers, latrines, and privies; gardens, vineyards, and orchards; ruins; ghettos; abandoned houses, those vandalized, or fallen into decay; mines, especially those of precious stones and metals; places where stagnant water collects; quicksand; muddy ground; stagnant or polluted lakes, ponds, swamps, rivers; brackish tidal basins; slaughterhouses; brothels; tombs; mausoleums; butcher shops. In houses: the drains, sinks, toilets; damp, moldy rooms that are shut off; any place that is secret or hidden, like secret stairs, underground tunnels, hidden doors; also secret drawers in desks or chests; any place used for hiding valuables. In real estate, it denotes slum property; swampy land with poor drainage; houses in bad repair; land in danger of flooding; land with unexploited mineral wealth or buried treasure; haunted houses, or those in lonely places with no easy access to them.

Among things, it signifies mineral wealth, buried treasure; swine; rats; vermin; birds of prey like eagles and those that eat carrion, like vultures; lobsters, shrimp, oysters, clams; dangerous sea creatures like sharks, octopuses, barracuda; street gangs; organized crime; secret negotiations; wrestling matches; judo; secret weapons; scientific research; archeology; piracy; dictatorships; scrap iron; sex; death; taxes; inheritance; welfare funds; annuities; pensions; debts; prostitution.

Among people and occupations, it rules surgeons; butchers; pimps; brothel keepers; prostitutes; gangsters; executioners; detectives; research scientists; archeologists; pirates; mercenary soldiers; nuclear physicists; sailors; naval officers; fruit growers; insurance brokers; social workers; undertakers; gynecologists; psychiatrists; vintners and wine merchants.

Among countries, it is said to rule the Barbary Coast, Morocco, Norway, Bavaria, Valencia and Catalonia in Spain. The city of Liverpool is said to be ruled by 19 Scorpio.

Its direction is north by east.

It is the fall of the Moon and the detriment of Venus. No planet is exalted here, although Uranus has a strong liking for the sign.

Sagittarius

Ruler: Jupiter *Quality*: Mutable *Element*: Fire

This ninth sign of the zodiac is hot, dry, barren, masculine, positive, diurnal, choleric, active; double-bodied, half human and half beast. It is sagacious, curious, exploratory, changeable, impatient of restraint, sociable, fun loving, witty, talkative, sportive, daring, optimistic, fickle, expansive, and superficial.

Its color is yellow-green, like chartreuse.

It rules the thighs and buttocks.

Among diseases, it signifies sciatica; falls from horses; injuries from large beasts; snake bites; afflictions caused by overexposure to extreme heat; hunting injuries; burns; malaria; sunstroke. Some areas of the sign are associated with blindness.

Among places it signifies stables; riding schools; race tracks; pasture for horses; universities; seminaries; publishers' offices; lawyers' offices; court rooms, especially those of the highest courts; privy council chambers; great houses with extensive grounds, like those of the nobility, or, in modern times, the very rich; places where clergymen live; cathedrals. In houses it rules upper rooms, balconies, areas close to the ceiling, and places near the fire. In real estate, it denotes open, hilly land, somewhat dry; the highest land around; mountain tops; hunting parks or grounds.

Among things it signifies horses and their gear; the metal tin and objects made of it; glass; religious artifacts and vestments; foreign countries; safaris, .hunting expeditions, and mountain climbing; publishing; commercial broadcasting; gambling; horse racing; lotteries; higher education; codes of law, ethics, or morality; long journeys; importing businesses; archery; philosophy; skyscrapers; high bridges; forest fires; the foreign policy of a country.

Among people and occupations it rules: foreigners; the clergy; scholars; philosophers; diplomats; the foreign service; gamblers; jockeys; horse breeders and trainers; world travelers; foreign correspondents; public relations; broadcasters'; publishers; lawyers; counselors to kings and presidents; gamblers; satirists; clowns; celibates; explorers; big game hunters; importers; philanderers; mountain climbers.

Among countries it is said to rule Spain, Arabia, Hungary, Yugoslavia; and the cities of Cologne, Budapest, Toledo in Spain.

Its direction is East by South.

It is the exaltation of the Moon's South Node, and the detriment of Mercury.

Capricorn

Ruler: Saturn   *Quality*: Cardinal   *Element*: Earth.

This tenth sign of the zodiac is cold, dry, melancholy, nocturnal, feminine, negative, pessimistic, bestial, practical, authoritarian, dutiful, narrow-minded, conservative, long-suffering, ambitious, status-conscious, resentful, malicious, unforgiving, selfish, miserly, coldly lecherous, political; a patient servant but a hard master.

Its colors are black and gray.

It rules the knees, teeth, skin, and skeleton of the body.

Among diseases, it signifies rheumatism and arthritis; osteomyelitis; psoriasis; deafness; leprosy; scurvy; rickets; eczema and other types of dermatitis; calcium deficiency diseases; tuberculosis of the bone; broken bones; curvature of the spine.

Among places it signifies stables for oxen, burros, mules or other work animals; goat sheds; barns for farm machinery; tanneries; manure piles and compost heaps; stone quarries; potteries; places where stone is cut or monuments are made; lead and zinc mines; woolen mills; police stations; night courts; magistrate courts; jury rooms; shoe stores or factories; places that make or sell leather objects like saddles, luggage, purses, leather garments; boundary lines, or the borders between countries; coal mines or places where coal is stored; diamond mines. In houses it denotes dark corners, dark places close to the ground, thresholds and places near them, and the foundations. Capricorn is the general significator of real estate, especially buildings of a solid, utilitarian, or commercial type. In rural land it indicates fallow or barren fields, cut-over timber land, or places overgrown with bushes and briars.

Among things it signifies hides, furs, woolens; lead; stone; slate; diamonds; coal; bones; rare woods like ebony and mahogany; wooden casks; sails; doors, gates, boundaries; the customs and its tariffs; anything made of lead, zinc, leather, bone, skin, shell, stone, or clay; bars, grilles, locks; rope, cords, string, chains; railroads; anything that confines or protects, like armor, corsets, belts; orthopedic equipment; crutches; passports; the estates of the dead; probate courts; any official documents relating to travel or the passage of goods between countries; funerals; mourning clothes, objects of somber hue, especially black; goats; crows, ravens; the foundations on which anything is built; corporations, especially those which are old, moribund, or monopolistic.

Among people and occupations it signifies all who work with leather, hides, wool; policemen; custom house officials; probate judges; estate administrators; dermatologists and bone surgeons; sail-makers; locksmiths; coopers; stone masons, bricklayers, cement workers; potters;

railroad men and truckers; diamond miners and merchants; lens grinders; contractors and builders of large, utilitarian or public buildings; all those who enforce discipline either publicly or privately, hence the mayor, the school principal, the governor, the business managers, the father in a family; misers; the old; chronic invalids.

Among countries it is said to rule India, Greece, parts of Persia (Iran), Lithuania, Saxony, Albania, Bulgaria, Mexico, Panama, the Orkney Islands; among towns, Oxford.

Its direction is south.

It is the exaltation of Mars, the detriment of the Moon, and the fall of Jupiter.

Aquarius

Ruler: Saturn (Uranus)   *Quality*: Fixed   *Element*: Air

This eleventh sign of the zodiac is hot, moist, airy, diurnal, masculine, sanguine, human, positive, nervous, active, talkative, inventive, democratic, reforming, scientific, dogmatic, intellectual, and argumentative. Its color is blue-green, like turquoise or aquamarine.

In answering questions by the horary method, Saturn should be used as the ruler of this sign. In the judgment of events and in mundane astrology, Uranus should be used.

It rules the calves and ankles, and the circulation of the blood. Among diseases it signifies weakness or crippling of the legs, leg cramps, broken or sprained ankles, circulatory disorders, diseases that are carried in the blood stream such as osteomyelitis, malaria, leukemia, and radiation poisoning.

Among places it signifies those that are hilly, uneven; newly excavated or freshly ploughed fields; great open holes, like quarries, especially of marble or limestone; archeological diggings. In houses, the roofs, especially if turreted or uneven; the eaves; rooms in turrets; widows' walks; high balconies; places built on roofs like pigeon cotes, pent-houses, air conditioning units, roof gardens; ventilators; places near windows which are drafty or airy. In real estate questions it rules hilly, windswept land; apartments or offices on upper floors; club houses or halls used for public meetings; property of interest to antiquarians; very modern houses using novel construction methods or materials.

Among things it signifies the winds; aircraft: parliaments; electronics; radio-activity; radium; x-rays; radios; telegraph; the metals aluminum and uranium; belfries; spires; lightning rods; clouds; kites; balloons; outer space and space research; physics; thermodynamics; astronomy; assemblies; labor unions; civil rights; adoption; hurricanes; riots; street demonstrations; antiques, especially old books; elections; sociology and social theory; revolution; social experiments; aviation and air lines; reorganization, especially of corporations; mergers and conglomerates; fraternal organizations like the Masons, Elks, Rotary clubs.

Among people and occupations it signifies aviators; elected representatives; astronauts; astronomers; physicists; sociologists; radio commentators and technicians; political orators; adopted children; revolutionaries; eccentric people, especially if old; reformers; labor organizers; collectors and curators of antiques and old books; people engaged in mass marketing, public relations, electioneering.

Among countries it is said to rule the Arabian Desert, Russia, Afghanistan, Tibet, Prussia, the parts of Poland bordering it, Lower Sweden. Among cities, Hamburg, Bremen, and probably Berlin and Moscow.

This sign has great effect upon the political affairs of England and the United States. Uranus in Aquarius coincides with wars, revolutions, territorial expansion and great changes in laws and government. It transited the sign in the 1830s, during World War I, and will do so again at the end of the century.

Its direction is west by north.

No planet is exalted in Aquarius. It is the detriment of the Sun.

Pisces

Ruler: Jupiter (Neptune) *Quality*: Mutable *Element*: Water

This twelfth sign of the zodiac is cold, fruitful, phlegmatic, feminine, negative, passive, double-bodied, idle, inactive, sickly, repressed, unfortunate, enslaved, hidden, indecisive, powerless, feeble, victimized. Its colors are gray-green and changeable pastels.

In horary questions, if the Moon, the significator of the querent or of the matter inquired about falls in Pisces, the chance of a favorable outcome is lessened. In an otherwise favorable chart, the benefits promised may be mixed with misfortune; or the matter may be more serious than appears on the surface. If the significator of an enemy or rival falls here, the misfortune is his and the prospects of .the querent are enhanced.

Pisces rules the feet, the liver, and the genes.

Among diseases, it signifies damage to the feet; gout; hepatitis; birth deformities; genetically transmitted diseases, like hemophilia or sickle cell anemia; also hereditary syphilis; damage to the embryo from drugs taken during pregnancy, or injuries caused during delivery; discharges of mucous or pus; poisoning; drug addiction; illness caused by overexposure to damp cold.

Among places it signifies flooded areas; ash ponds; swamps; rivers; tidal basins; the ocean; moats; wells. In general, it denotes standing water, while Cancer means running water. It also signifies hospitals; jails; orphanages; monasteries; convents; insane asylums; places of retirement; junk yards; slave quarters; dungeons; stockades or any place where people or animals are kept against their wills; penal colonies; ghettos; concentration or prison camps. In real estate questions, it warns one to be extremely cautious, for it denotes property liable to flooding, poorly drained, swampy, or subject to noxious fumes. If in cities, ghetto property, places in declining neighborhoods, slums, condemned buildings, or hangouts for criminals. In all real estate transactions, it warns of clouded titles, declining values, or the possibility of fraud.

Among things it signifies fog; chemicals; poisons; drugs; oil; fish and the mammals of the sea; the ocean, especially its mysterious depths; liquor; espionage; chemistry; photography; motion pictures; the ballet; occultism; psychic phenomena; piracy; junk; anything discarded, unwanted; trash heaps; unsolved mysteries; ghosts; specters, whether real or imaginary; hallucinations, especially if caused by drugs or alcohol; suicide; skeletons in the family closet; dreams; the subconscious; sleep; what happened before one was born; mysticism; Christianity; martyrdom.

Among people and occupations it rules chemists; sailors; liquor merchants; monks; nuns; those who work in hospitals, jails, orphanages; psychoanalysts; junk dealers; scavengers; drug addicts and pushers; alcoholics; neurotics; prisoners; slaves; all who are in bondage or exploited; the secret enemy; secret agents; fishermen; divers; dancers; foundlings; illegitimate children; clairvoyants.

Among countries, it is said to rule Portugal, the Normandy Coast, Galicia in Spain; and among cities Alexandria and Seville.

Its direction is north by west.

It is the exaltation of Venus and the fall of Mercury.

5

The Old Planets

In horary astrology the planets never represent subjective conditions, abstract values, or general principles, as they do in natal astrology. The horary chart cannot be used as a basis for ethical judgments. It will never tell us whether a project is right or wrong, but only whether it will succeed or fail. The saint may die, the assassin may succeed, the tyrant may conquer, and the innocent may be convicted—all without any consideration of the ethical values involved or the right and wrong of the matter.

The system provides guidance in material, practical, mundane affairs. If no abstract values are read into the chart, it will tell us facts which, at the moment of asking the question, are still unknown to us. Facts are always neutral. Once we know them, we form value judgments and make decisions on the basis of them. These values and decisions are not in the horary chart itself.

Like facts, the planets are neutral. They are called "significators." They represent things, people, parts of the body, occupations, and physical conditions. They describe, they do not evaluate. Since each planet represents many different things, it is necessary to select the one pertinent to the question, which is always limited in its scope. Many possible meanings are immediately eliminated because they have no relevance to the question.

We then consider the *sign* the planet falls in. This gives us information about its condition; and once more many possibilities are eliminated because they are irrelevant. We then consider the *house* the planet falls in, which will describe the circumstances in which that person or thing (the planet) finds itself at the moment, and still more possibilities are eliminated.

By this process we are merely gathering facts descriptive of a person, thing, or situation. So far, all we are concerned with is whether they pertain to the question, and not at all with whether the significator is a so-called malefic or benefic. Jupiter may signify a thief, Saturn a beloved child, which only means that Jupiter will tell us pertinent facts about the thief, such as where he is hiding, who his associates are, what he's done with the loot; and Saturn will tell us pertinent facts about the child.

Every planet has its own brand of benefits and disasters; of virtues and vices; of health and disease. What it will confer upon us depends solely upon its situation by sign, house, and *aspects* as these are revealed by each question. For instance, Saturn rules lead; the Sun rules gold. Most people consider gold more desirable than lead. That is an abstract value judgment which may be contrary to the facts elicited from a particular chart drawn to answer a question about investments. If Saturn is strong by sign, house, and aspects, the querent may make a fortune in lead. If the Sun is weak by sign, house, and afflicted by aspects, he may lose his shirt in gold.

A planet is always itself and behaves like itself. It is a dynamic force that carries the action of the house and sign it rules or occupies into other sections of the chart where it has the power to influence the course of events through its position or aspects. This influence is *always* symbolic of its own nature. It acts upon a house and through a sign because these furnish its environment at the moment. The house provides the *circumstances* through which it acts. The sign provides the *atmosphere* that surrounds it. But no matter what the circumstances or atmosphere, it will never act like another planet in the same circumstances or atmosphere. Just as a human being retains his own identity from the cradle to the grave, through all circumstances and environments, so does a planet. You may live in another man's house all your life, but you can never become that man, even if his house is a prison. In fact, you may, through your influence, change the atmosphere of his house; but if so, it will only be in ways compatible with your own powers. You can never do this by using means incompatible with your own nature and identity, for these are not available to you.

For example, if Jupiter, the great benefic, happens to be the significator of death in a horary chart, it will kill in the manner of Jupiter, through a Jupiter disease or through excess, overoptimism, improvidence. The same is true if it is a significator of loss. If Saturn is the significator of wealth or fame, it will gain these *only* by Saturnian means—through hard work, dogged persistence, learning by experience, and political acumen. By nature, Jupiter is lucky and Saturn is not. But luck is fickle and experience is not. Many a famous criminal was born with Jupiter in the tenth house: an indication of his notoriety, not of his wisdom. Very few famous criminals were born with Saturn in the tenth for such people are, in the main, too pessimistic about their careers to believe they can get by with murder.

In answering questions by the horary method, I find that better results are generally obtained by using the traditional sign rulerships. This ancient scheme is:

	Ruler		
Positive			*Negative*
Leo	Sun	Moon	Cancer
Gemini	Mercury		Virgo
Libra	Venus		Taurus
Aries	Mars		Scorpio
Sagittarius	Jupiter		Pisces
Aquarius	Saturn		Capricorn

In such charts, the three outer planets—Uranus, Neptune, and Pluto—may furnish valuable corroborative evidence about the matter. They seem to indicate people or conditions that exist outside the orbit of the question, but which may nevertheless affect it in ways beyond the querent's control. They represent factors in the social environment or in the natural world which will operate in their own fashion regardless of what the querent does. The chart will indicate whether these uncontrollable factors will help *or* hinder the querent's project, but it is usually impossible to foresee *how* they will help or hinder because they are operating in a frame of reference inaccessible to the querent. This is because the question concerns an intimate, personal problem, which, even if it looms large to him, is but a tiny fragment of all human and natural activity going forward in the world at that time.

Just as King Canute could not stop the tides, he cannot stop an earthquake, a war, or the actions of people unknown who may nevertheless affect his project in some unforeseen way. The way will always be unforeseen because the querent is unaware of the external forces involved, and he is not in a position to get enough information about them to bring their activity into the orbit of his consciousness.

A horary chart is a diagram of the querent's *awareness,* conscious, and subconscious, at the moment he asks the question. Anything of which he is wholly *unaware* at that moment, but which will affect the outcome, will manifest in the chart as a mysterious, unpredictable force. The three outer planets are useful to indicate where such forces will act, and, through the aspects they receive, whether their action will help or hinder the project. If these planets are used to rule Aquarius, Pisces, and Scorpio, respectively, this additional insight is lost.

Usually if an outer planet posts a warning signal, the traditional rulers will give a negative answer, but not always. Sometimes the traditional rulers give a favorable answer, but a badly afflicted outer planet intervenes. This usually means that the idea is a good one, but that an unpredictable disaster will intervene to prevent its consummation. The querent should then hold off until after the disaster occurs. He may find that previously unknown features have been revealed, and that knowing them changes the focus of the problem, so that he can use the same idea, but in a slightly different and more advantageous way.

Here is an example of this method of using the outer planets. In a chart drawn to answer a question about the wisdom of opening a bank account in a foreign country, Pluto fell in the second house, which always represents the querent's money. It was retrograde at the end of Virgo, in a trine aspect to Saturn. Before this trine became exact, however, Pluto would change direction and move into Libra. This said, very clearly, that something was going on behind the scenes concerning vast wealth (Pluto); and that whatever it was would come out in the open when the trine was formed in Gemini (news) and Libra (compromise, treaties, agreements). Right on time, the news appeared: devaluation of the dollar. Notice that Pluto's modern rulership of Scorpio provided additional clues. In the natural zodiac, Scorpio is the sign of other people's money, of the resources of a nation's allies, of loss through elimination, and of mysterious manipulations behind the scenes.

In the judgment of events, where a chart is set up for the moment something happens, and you want to know how this event will affect you, whether or not you use the outer planets as sign rulers depends upon their relevance to the matter. For example, suppose you are offered a job with an airline. You set up a chart for the moment you receive the offer. Aquarius falls on the sixth house of employment. Uranus rules air lines. Therefore it, and not Saturn, should be used as the ruler of Aquarius in this case. Even if Aquarius fell on some other house less obviously involved with the matter, Uranus should still be used as its ruler because in such cases it ceases to be an uncontrollable social factor and becomes the neutral significator of the matter in question.

In another case, a chemist received an offer from the Navy to do top-secret research on missile fuels. The chart set up for the moment he received the offer had Neptune exactly rising in Scorpio. Neptune rules chemistry, the Navy, secrecy, and missile fuels. Scorpio signifies scientific research, especially that concerning new sources of power or wealth. Therefore, Neptune should be used as the neutral ruler of Pisces and Pluto of Scorpio. These two planets were then in a close sextile with the Jupiter-Saturn conjunction in Capricorn trine Pluto and sextile Neptune. He was advised to take the job and subsequently invented new fuels that were vital to our space ventures.

But suppose the event had been different. Suppose he had seen a house at that moment and asked about the wisdom of buying it. Uranus, Neptune, and Pluto have no relevance to real estate questions, Therefore, Mars becomes the ruler of the Ascendant (the buyer), Saturn (real estate) becomes the ruler of Aquarius on the fourth (the property). These two planets were in bad aspect to each other, and Mars was also in bad aspect to Venus, ruler of the seventh (the seller). This man would be advised not to buy the house because the significators of the matter were too adverse. But Neptune rising gives a clue as to *why* they were adverse: he would become the victim of criminal fraud or of social circumstances involving many people, and he would never be able to recover his losses.

In the first case, the bad condition of Mars indicated the extreme danger of the work, of which the client was well aware anyhow. In the second case, with Mars the chart ruler, the whole proposition becomes destructive to the client and would offer him no advantage. Yet, we are looking at the *same chart*. The answers are different because the two events are different and call for different significators. Here, as with everything else in astrology, it is necessary to use commonsense.

In mundane charts that concern the fate of nations, the outer planets should always be used as rulers of Aquarius, Pisces, and Scorpio.

Moon

The Moon signifies the following things and conditions:

Function: how well or badly anything works, including the physiology of the body.

Time: in all horary questions, and usually in the judgment of events, the Moon is the measure of time, which is calculated according to the formula in Chapter 9. In mundane charts, the movement of planets to eclipse points or to angles and the transits over them may be more accurate.

Imagination: psychosomatic diseases or physiological malfunctioning in which the imagination or subconscious mind plays a great part.

Fertility

Assimilation, especially of nourishment. The Moon rules the stomach.

Eyeglasses, or any surface that reflects an image; transient opinions, borrowed light, reflected glory. This reflecting capacity causes us to say that the Moon *carries* the light from one planet to the next in a horary chart, while she herself remains neutral.

The tides, hence, anything that operates with a regular ebb and flow.

The mother, wife, female children, or any woman inquired about.

Servants

Anything commonplace.

Embryos, or anything that is forming in embryo.

The missing person, animal, or thing.

Silver, pearls and many semiprecious stones that are milky or green in color, like moonstones, jade, feldspar.

In mundane charts, the Moon rules *the People,* hence, in both natal and horary work, it has a bearing on public opinion.

Sun

The Sun signifies the following things and conditions:

The vitality of the organism, hence, the *viability* of the matter in question. A weak, afflicted Sun in a horary chart usually indicates that the question is not important, that the matter lacks the vitality to endure.

The heart, both of the body and of the matter.

The father, husband, lover. Any male in a position of authority over one, such as an employer or boss.

In mundane charts, the Sun rules the king, the president, the dictator, or anyone else serving as the head of a nation. It also rules the Pope.

Mercury

Mercury signifies the following things and conditions:

Communication, hence, written and spoken words and all languages, messages, rumors, the news.

Logic, hence, mathematics, scientific-reasoning, and rational thought. Therefore, a badly afflicted Mercury in a horary chart indicates a person whose mental processes are disordered or irrational; or one who lies or spreads false rumors.

Documents, hence, all licenses, records, deeds, manuscripts, letters, patents.

Messengers and couriers

Inventors

Commuters and the *vehicles* that carry them, hence, automobiles, bicycles, and buses.

Pickpockets and *forgers*

The hands, arms, and intestinal tract

Merchants and traders

In mundane charts, Mercury, as ruler of Gemini, signifies elementary and high schools; children and young people; messengers; the news media; all gadgets in daily use. As ruler of Virgo, it signifies the armed forces, the civil service, libraries, computers, the personal diet, and food supplies of the nation.

Venus

Venus signifies the following things and conditions:

The *sweetheart* or *mistress*, hence, a man's general sexual attitude toward women and the nature of his sexual relations with them.

Social relations, hence, parties and anything done to promote amiability and to make things run smoothly.

Partnerships

Marriages

Contracts, legal or social

Arts and handcrafts, hence, anything that embellishes the environment and makes life more elegant or gracious.

Young women

Money, jewelry, valuable *artifacts*

Copper and bronze and things made of them.

Purses, safes, safe deposit boxes.

People working in the decorative arts, hence, dressmakers, hairdressers, interior and landscape designers, jewelers, and florists.

The kidneys and lower back

The neck and throat, hence, singers and choirs.

Adversely connected with the sign Scorpio or its rulers, Venus may indicate venereal disease.

Its colors are azure blue and pastel hues.

In mundane astrology, Venus, as ruler of Libra, signifies peace, treaties, allies, courts of law, the public streets, and museums.

If badly afflicted, it signifies war, civil strife, enemies of the State, and bad alliances. As ruler of Taurus, it signifies banks, the stock exchange, commodity and cattle markets, cattle ranches, and those resources of the nation that are in the hands of the people. When badly afflicted by Pluto, Uranus, or Neptune, Venus in a mundane chart may prophesy plagues or epidemics, especially influenza. By Saturn, it may indicate corruption in the courts or poverty among the people.

Mars

Mars signifies the following things and conditions:

Energy, hence, engines and all types of machines that produce energy.

Initiative

The male sex drive

The head, the brain as an organ of the body, and *the sex organs.*

Accidents, especially those that result in bleeding.

Soldiers

Pioneers

Engineers

Weapons, especially those carried in the hand that inflicts cuts or wounds, such as guns, swords, and knives.

Strife, dissension, arguments

Warlike games, or *contests of athletic prowess.*

Hunters

Sheep, lambs, and those who raise or herd them.

The process of elimination, especially by death or violence.

Fevers

Surgeons and surgery

In questions about health, if Venus is also badly *afflicted,* it may indicate venereal disease.

Its colors are red and purple.

It rules iron and steel, and all things made of these metals.

In mundane charts, Mars, as ruler of Aries, signifies war, violent crime, soldiers in combat, the steel industry, arsenals, colonizing new territory. As ruler of Scorpio, it signifies death, carnage, crime waves, taxes, the nation's intelligence service, policemen in vice squads and homicide divisions (detectives), torture chambers or camps, organized crime, and the resources of the nation's allies or enemies.

Jupiter

Jupiter signifies the following things and conditions:

Expansion

Luck, hence, prizes and awards; *gamblers and gambling*

Horse racing, rate tracks, and racing stables

Travel to foreign countries, hence, foreigners and strangers one meets, even at home.

Churches and clergymen

Lawyers and judges

One's code of honor or ethics

Universities

Philosophers and philosophy

Publishers and publishing

Large wild animals, hence, zoos and game preserves

Mountains and mountain climbers

People of high status, great fame, or national importance

A badly afflicted Jupiter may indicate fame through crime or dishonor.

Lavish expenditure, hence, if afflicted, extravagance or loss through reckless speculation or gambling.

Tin and tin mines, articles made of tin

Its colors are yellow-green and aquamarine.

Jupiter rules the liver, the thighs and the buttocks, hence, when afflicted, it describes diseases and injuries of these parts.

In mundane astrology, Jupiter, as ruler of Sagittarius, signifies the foreign service, the nobility, the nation's highest court, universities, churches, the clergy, the counselors to the king or president, foreign relations, and foreign countries; the cultural and moral traditions of the nation, the honor of the country. As ruler of Pisces, it signifies hospitals, penal institutions, monasteries, secret negotiations, secret enemies, espionage, naval strength, charitable institutions.

In mundane charts concerning war, Jupiter's placement may indicate which side will be victorious. For instance, when the Japanese bombed Pearl Harbor, Jupiter was in Gemini, transiting the first house of the United States' horoscope. It was retrograde, however, assuring an American victory. Even so, the United States was ill-prepared and got off to a slow start.

In 1939, when Hitler started WW II, it was in Aries, transiting the first house of the British national chart (1066). Saturn, significator of defeat, was in Taurus, transiting the first house of the German national chart (1871). In 1941, when Hitler invaded Russia, Jupiter was in Taurus and Gemini, in Germany's first house, but Saturn was also there, which could be read: initial German victories, but eventual defeat.

In 1967, when the Six Day War broke out in the Middle East, Jupiter was in Cancer, transiting Israel's tenth house, another position assuring victory.

In 1914, at the outbreak of WW I, it was in Aquarius, transiting the United States tenth. We did not declare war on Germany until April 1917, when Jupiter was in Taurus. By August, when American participation became active, it had moved into Gemini, once more assuring an American victory.

Notice that for this type of quick analysis of the probable outcome of wars, it is necessary to have correct, workable birth charts for at least one of the nations involved. Unfortunately, these are rare. If they are unobtainable, the chart of the nation's ruler may be substituted. Thus, in 1939, Jupiter in Aries transited Hitler's seventh house: victory to his enemies. In 1967, when it was in Cancer, it transited Gamal Nasser's seventh: victory to Egypt's enemies.

In event charts, we can read Jupiter in the same way. If it appears in the first or tenth house, it means triumph for the person or group initiating the action. If it appears in the seventh or fourth, his adversaries will probably win.

This quick method is not infallible. The Jupiter may be retrograde or so afflicted or weak by sign and the Saturn so strong, even though not angular, as to make the victory too costly to pursue. You can win the lawsuit, but lose a fortune; get hold of the property but be unable to pay off the mortgage; sign the contract only to find your new partners are dishonest.

Therefore, although Jupiter is always a protective and benefic influence when it falls in the house signifying the matter under question, clients should not be advised to pursue their project on this testimony alone. The whole chart must be studied carefully, especially the condition of the Moon. None of the strictures against judgment can be ignored merely because Jupiter is angular.

Saturn

Saturn signifies the following things and conditions:

Limitation

Frustration

Want, lack, hardship, privation

Boundaries, the outer *limits* of property and, in mundane charts, of the nation; in questions of morality, the *limits* of socially or legally permissible conduct.

Loss

Real estate, especially large utilitarian buildings like offices, factories, warehouses.

Foundations, especially of buildings; but if the interpretation demands, it can also signify the foundation of the State (the American Constitution), a family (the founding father), a great financial reserve (the Rockefeller or Ford Foundations).

The skeleton of the body, hence, all bones and things made of them.

The teeth

Armor

The Skin, which is the boundary or outer limits of the body; hence, animal hides, leather, shells, which are the armor of some sea creatures and reptiles.

Whatever *binds,* like rope, cord, chains.

Whatever *smothers,* like feathers, blankets.

Strangulation, choking

Fails, either physical or from power.

Ambition and the hard work that achieves it.

Fear, hence, Saturn in the proper context may become a significator of *paranoia.*

Extreme cold, hence, whatever protects us from it, like woolens, overcoats, and furs.

The metal lead and things made of it.

The color black and hues so dark they shade into black.

Corporations

The chief executive, hence, a significator of the father, the chairman of the board, and in mundane work, the administration.

Discipline and whoever enforces it, like the police, the long arm of the law, the judge in a courtroom, the warden in a prison, or the father.

Funerals and what pertains to them: mourning, hearses, undertakers, cemeteries, coffins.

India and its people.

Coal, coal mines, and miners.

Carbon, hence, *diamonds*.

Very old people or things

Puritans and puritanism

Goats

Blunt instruments, hence, hammers, cudgels, clubs

Karma, hence, the reward or punishment due one's merits or misdeeds

Time

Weight, weighing machines, or anything excessively *heavy*

Because Saturn embodies the principles of limitation, inhibition, and discipline, it has a restraining effect upon the pure activity or nature of the other planets. It chills the ardor of the Sun, frustrates the recklessness of Mars, inhibits the sociability of Venus, makes the Moon fearful of emotion, curtails the flightiness of Mercury, and sharply limits the expansion of Jupiter.

Since Jupiter and Saturn express two opposite principles, their conjunctions, which occur every twenty years, are extremely important in mundane astrology. They indicate a *reversal of trend* in mundane affairs because the Jupiter influence expands blindly in a given direction until it suddenly meets Saturn, which stops its forward march like an insurmountable stone wall. That is why charts drawn for these conjunctions are called *Mutations,* which means *change*. For 240 years, these conjunctions occur in the same element and are called *Lesser Mutations*. When the conjunction moves from one element into another, the change is called the *Great Mutation*. The last Great Mutation occurred in 1842, when the conjunctions moved from the fire into the earth element.

The Great Mutation horoscope is the master chart for a long cycle in world affairs. Adjusted for the capital of any nation, it can be progressed by solar arc to warn against forthcoming crises in that nation's historical development. As events occur, their importance to the nation can be judged against this background.

In American politics, Saturn rules the Democratic Party because it is the older, and Jupiter rules the Republicans. The Great Mutation of 1842 occurred in the ninth degree of Capricorn, falling in the eighth house (death) of our national chart. Since then every president elected or inaugurated in the year of the Lesser Mutation has died in office. These deaths symbolize changes in the internal structure of American affairs and in our status as a world power. They are often connected with the end or beginning of wars as well as with more subtle changes. For example:

1840 (Harrison). The period to 1860 was marked by great territorial expansion after the Mexican War and the annexation of Texas and California.

1860 (Lincoln). The period to 1880 was marked by the Civil War, the end of black slavery, and the end of political domination by the agricultural South.

1880 (Garfield). The period to 1900 was marked by the end of the Indian Wars, closing of the Frontier, the rise of corporations, and the beginning of political domination by the industrial North.

1900 (McKinley). The period to 1920 was marked by the end of the Spanish-American War. First overseas possessions, the rise of America as a world power, and construction of the Panama Canal.

1920 (Harding). The period to 1940 was marked by the end of WW I, which closed an era. Isolationism, collapse of the economy, depression, prohibition, and the rise of organized crime.

1940 (Roosevelt). The period to 1960 was marked by WW II, great expansion of the prestige and world power of the U.S., and the beginning of the Welfare State.

1960 (Kennedy). The period to 1980 was marked by Vietnam, uncontrolled lawlessness (street crime), and increasing disillusionment with foreign involvement. Racial warfare (riots), beginning in the 1960s, was an important features of the era.

1980 (Reagan). In 1980, there was an aberration in the conjunction, which occurred in Libra, an air sign. It fell in the fifth house of our national chart, square our Jupiter-Venus conjunction in Cancer. Ronald Reagan was shot in 1981 but survived.

2000 (George W. Bush). The mutation conjunction was in an earth sign. The Al Qaeda attack on the U.S. (9/11) occurred during his presidency.

6

The New Planets

When answering personal questions by horary astrology, better results are usually obtained by using the classical rulers of the signs Aquarius, Scorpio, and Pisces. This leaves Uranus, Pluto, and Neptune free to signify special conditions existing in the social world beyond the control of the querent, but which may still affect the outcome in unexpected ways. Or the outer planets may be used to signify things, conditions, or people which they rule specifically. I find that using the outer planets in this fashion gives extra depth to the chart and greater insight into its meaning.

But an increasing number of competent horary astrologers prefer to use the outer planets as exclusive rulers of Aquarius, Scorpio, and Pisces. I suggest the student experiment with both methods and settle for the one that works best for him or her. Oddly enough, if both methods are tested on the same chart, they will usually yield the same answer.

Uranus

Uranus signifies the following things and conditions:

The principle of reorganization; hence, any sudden disturbance or wreckage of the status quo that makes reorganization inevitable.

Reformation, particularly social or political, through violence.

Revolutions, particularly those in which kings and aristocracies are overthrow.

The circulation of the blood; hence, the sudden onset of many blood-born diseases.

The circulation of the news; hence, the mass media and the technical inventions that made telegraphs, telephones, radio, and television possible. This is communication at a distance from a central control with those who receive the news and are unable to answer back. It must be distinguished from the *personal* give and take of Mercury's communication. The telephone as a gadget in common use that permits a personal verbal interchange is ruled by Mercury. The technology that makes telephones possible and its use by the mass media are Uranian.

The circulation of the wind; hence, violent storms, hurricanes, and tornados.

Reformers; hence, all *utopian ideologies* that aim to reform man into a perfect social being.

Corporations and all associations of equals who are powerless alone, but when united, can become a dominant force—labor unions, parliaments, congresses, professional associations.

The common man, en masse. This meaning comes from Aquarius, the sign opposite Leo, the king: that is, all the other people who are not kings and are, therefore, commoners.

Eccentric people, particularly if old and crotchety.

Outer space and its exploration.

Astronomy. Uranus is also given the rulership of astrology, but long observation and testing has made me somewhat doubtful of this. In the charts of astrologers, their clients, and students of astrology, I find Jupiter and Sagittarius emphasized more strongly and frequently than Aquarius and Uranus. Indeed, all the Fire signs seem to be overemphasized in astrologer's charts, but more work would have to be done on this before we can be certain.

The Industrial Revolution. This coincided with the discovery of Uranus in 1781. It ushered in the Age of Technology, ruled by Uranus. Therefore, Uranus rules *heavy industry*, the machinery it uses, the rationalized factory system, and the mass production this system made possible. Whenever anything is done in the name of the masses—mankind, in general—look to Uranus as the possible ruler. Thus, it rules mass production, mass media, the universal franchise, the Rights of Man, all parliaments, congresses, assemblies that allegedly speak for the masses, and Civil Rights. Social and political theories of a rational, secular nature, which purport to serve *humanity as a whole* and are, therefore, said to be *humanitarian,* are ruled by Uranus. In this context, do not confuse the Uranian masses (all mankind) with the Proletariat, a special class ruled by Neptune but included in the Uranian mass. Uranian "humanity" excludes only kings and aristocrats, and even these may come into the mass once Uranian revolution has reduced them to a common status.

Electricity and electrical energy, radium and radioactivity

X-ray. In questions about health, this includes x-ray and radium treatment.

Earthquakes; explosions

Homosexuality and social issues related to it.

Castration, and neuroses related to the "castration complex."

This rulership relates to the myth about the ancient sky god Uranus, who was castrated and robbed of his power by his son Chronos (Saturn).

The nervous system, especially those nerves that control the motor reflexes.

Heavy artillery, the kind now called "conventional" as against "atomic" weapons.

Aircraft and spacecraft

The unexpected and unforeseeable. Such events may be monumental disasters, amazing good fortune, or a combination of both. Their effect is to revolutionize the life or the society in some unexpected way.

In considerations of Uranus and its influence, remember that its action is extreme and of a back-lash type. It brings benefit from disaster, and disaster from what seems like incredible good luck. It may promise freedom and bring tyranny, as in the French Revolution. Promise the fulfillment of all needs through industrial production and bring destruction of the environment through industrial wastes. Promise freedom from feudal lords and bring slavery under industrial lords. Its promises are noble, but when fulfilled, they turn mysteriously into their opposites.

Be wary of Uranus bearing gifts. It is the reformer who loves humanity and hates people. It deals in abstractions—the larger the better.

In personal questions, it frequently indicates a break in some important relationship: divorce, partnerships, broken contracts, children leaving home, sudden death of someone dear to the querent.

Uranus rules the metals aluminum and uranium. Its color is sky blue.

Uranus is exactly rising in our Declaration of Independence chart. It is, therefore, the ruling planet of the United States.

Neptune

Neptune signifies the following things and conditions: *the principle of diffusion*.

Neptune is the most difficult of all planets to understand because its mode of operation is so subtle and so slow as to be imperceptible on the material and rational planes where human judgments are formed. Abstractly, Neptune is the astrological analogue of the Second Law of Thermodynamics in physics: that is, the principle of *entropy*. Entropy is the process by which a given amount of energy, when released into the environment, gradually becomes diluted or diffused throughout the entire available area until it appears to be dissolved in its surroundings. The total amount of energy released remains the same, but as it is diffused through the widest possible area it merges so completely with its surroundings that it cannot be retrieved in its original form. Its power becomes so diluted, vitiated, that it loses its original integrity and turns into something else. Anyone can demonstrate how this works by taking a gallon jug of clear water and placing a drop of ink in it. In a minute or less, the ink will disappear, dissolved in the water, although, it will still be there. You can now take the gallon of water and dump it in the river, where it will immediately blend with the stream, but the ink will still be there. The river will dump your water into the ocean. The ink will still be there, but who can now recognize it, much less retrieve it?

This law, stated in religious terms, forms the basis of the philosophy of the Upanishads. This, and all similar religious philosophies that teach that the One (individual ego) must merge with the will (cosmic consciousness) and become an irretrievable part of it, are ruled by Neptune. The goal of all religious mysticism (ruled by Neptune) is the loss of the individual ego, which, by losing its identity as a separate I, merges with the universal, immortal mind of Brahma. The individual soul then experiences the paradox of finding its Self through losing itself (ego). This is the meaning of the words of Jesus: "I and my Father are One."

Since all planets operate in the same way on all levels of human experience from the highest to the lowest, according to the nature of the planet, Neptune rules everything associated with the loss of individual identity, with the dissolution of the ego, with the merging of the individual thing or person into an amorphous collection or collective.

Therefore it rules:

Communism, the political ideology that would merge the individual into the proletarian mass.

Junk, where the original integrity of things is lost through breakage, wear and tear, or dissolution.

Self-sacrifice

Christianity, the religion that worships the Son of God made flesh so that He could sacrifice Himself for the salvation of mankind.

Slavery and slaves

Impotence, whether physical, mental, or spiritual; hence, those rendered powerless to act as integrated individuals through severe illness, privation, insanity, alcohol, or drugs. This meaning derives from Neptune's subtle insistence upon the loss or sacrifice of some if part of the self, or of self-awareness. All types of impotence are humiliations of the ego.

Dreams, images, mirages, hallucinations. Neptune rules all evanescent, ephemeral visions that convey a false picture of reality or seek to convince us that something actually non-existent in the material sense does have a tangible, physical body; hence, photography, motion pictures, television, public image, propaganda, and many types of fraud.

Deception. When Neptune forms an adverse aspect to the planet ruling the querent or to the one ruling the matter asked about, it is safe to assume some degree of deception, delusion, or fraud is operating, and that it is connected with the house and sign in which Neptune is placed. Unfortunately, the querent will seldom believe warnings about this because when Neptune is involved, the victim cooperates in the deception: he has lost control over some facet of his ego. He has sacrificed some of his autonomy to Neptune, and that lost part of the self *wants* to be deceived. Most Neptunian frauds succeed because they promise the victim something he wants: pie in the sky, instant wealth, or easy fame. Neptune's schemes feed on the victim's greed, on his own dishonesty, or upon his desire to present a false front to the world. Neptune cannot deceive an honest man, but who among us is always honest, especially with himself? Saints and mystics, ruled by Neptune, give up the world and all worldly desires to avoid becoming the victims of this negative side of their ruling planet.

Poisons, drugs, and alcohol.

Welfare and charity, and the institutions or groups that dispense them.

Orphans and orphanages, illegitimate children.

Skeletons in the family closet or anything in one's personal life that is kept hidden from the world through a strong sense of shame, and to some extent forces a person to live a lie.

Embezzlement

Bankruptcy

On the material or constructive side, Neptune rules:

The ocean, hence, ships, navies, sailors

Hospitals

Chemistry and chemists

Gas and oil

Fish, fishermen, fishmongers

The ballet and ballet dancers

Poets, painters, musicians

The endocrine glands and the chemistry of the body

Salt

Pearls, coral, and other wealth of the sea

Its colors are sea-green and iridescent, pearl-like hues.

In mundane astrology, Neptune rules the Navy, the nation's hospitals and welfare programs, counter-espionage, the prison system, secret enemies, political propaganda, chemical warfare, social problems concerning drugs, prostitution, persecuted minorities, vandalism, inflated money, gigantic fraudulent schemes. In nations that have them, it rules serfs, slaves, and peons—all types of conscripted labor. Also in nations that have them, it rules concentration camps and POW camps. It is a factor in the pollution of the environment, especially of rivers and streams and by smog, smoke, and fumes. In mundane charts concerning the assassination of a public figure, Neptune rules the assassin.

Modern American astrologers give the rulership of the Black race to Neptune, probably because of their previous history, in the United States, of slavery, ostracism, and disadvantage. But about a year ago I was the only white person on a television panel with three educated black men who wanted to discuss astrology. One of these men took violent exception to the assignment of Neptune as ruler of the blacks. He said that everything Neptune stood for was negative, demeaning, and insulting to his people: it was a crude example, he said, of racism applied to astrology. He said that a black astrologer of his acquaintance claimed that the Moon, not Neptune, ruled the Negro race; and that until white astrologers recognized this, they could never begin to understand the blacks.

Since then I have thought a lot about this idea, and I've concluded there is much to be said for it. First, we should remember that the general Neptune rulership of slaves, serfs, the persecuted, and the sorely disadvantaged has nothing to do with race or nationality. Throughout history people of all faces and nations have, at times, been enslaved, usually by their own kind. In fact, until the end of the 18th century, the lowest class in all societies always existed in some sort of bondage: slavery, serfdom, or conscripted labor. Neptune rules this *condition of bondage,* whether the people involved are black, white, yellow, red, poor, illiterate, or wise. Kings, aristocrats, heretics, political enemies, and beggars are all ruled by Neptune while they are in bondage. Once released, however, and put back in control of their own lives, they are not. As astrologers, we must be careful not to confuse the rulership of a temporary condition with the individual himself or with the nation he belongs to.

Second, from very ancient times, the entire continent of Africa has been assigned to the rulership of the Moon. Egypt, the only great civilization that was exclusively African, was a matriarchy to the end; and there are many other facets of life, culture, and thought that indicate a lunar orientation. Islam, which has been the dominant African civilization for over a thousand years, is a Moon-ruled religion and culture. The tribal organization of black Africa, which is only now beginning to break up, is a Moon-ruled social system. Why then, if the blacks themselves feel that they are a lunar people, should we argue with them? The experienced astrologer knows very well the nature of the Moon, how it functions, and its relationship to the Earth. Using this knowledge he should observe his fellow citizens without prejudice to see if their collective behavior, chosen way of life and their vision of cultural ideals are indeed lunar. And we should certainly listen to black astrologers and pay attention to what they say about their people, because people do understand themselves.

If you don't believe this is true, practice astrology for a few years. You will find that you can never tell a client anything about himself that he doesn't know already, in his heart.

Nothing is more important in astrology than the assignment of correct rulerships. It takes many years, even centuries, of observation to arrive at correct judgments. In the case of the outer planets, we may be making mistakes solely because we have not observed them for long enough. Neptune is undoubtedly one of the most powerful planetary forces in the solar system. It pervades everything, subverts everything, influences everything and, in the end, takes a subtle inner command over everything. It does this because it is the planetary symbol of what Carl Jung called the Collective Unconscious. During the Piscean Age, Neptune produced two great religions: Christianity and Buddhism. Through the dominance of these religions, it produced great civilizations in Europe, Byzantium, southern India, and eastern Asia, together with a large number of important subcultures. Neptune strives for universality and collectivism; the Moon strives for a closed, familial system. These are opposites. It is impossible that they should rule the same things or be confused for long in their proper functions.

Neptune does rule the State of Israel, which was founded May 14, 1948, at 4:00 p.m., Tel Aviv Summer Time. Neptune, at 10 Libra, is exactly rising, giving it the same type of dominance over the Israel chart that Uranus has over the chart of the United States.

Pluto

Pluto signifies the following things and conditions:

The principle of metamorphosis

Pluto, Lord of the Underworld, rules everything that takes refuge, or is buried, in the ground for a certain season, then emerges in a different visible form; hence, *Seeds, spermatozoa and ova.*

The hidden wealth in mines.

Any phase of the growth cycle that is hidden from view, such as *incubation and the chrysalis.*

The concept described in the myth of the Phoenix, where a new creature is reborn from the ashes of a dead life; that is, *Karma.*

Death and regeneration

Snakes, which shed their skins to emerge bright and new looking. The armored reptiles that have survived from ancient ages: *crocodiles, iguanas, armadillos, lizards, and turtles.*

Vultures and other birds that eat carrion.

Corpses

Buried treasure

Sex and the *sex organs* of all species in which males and females are differentiated from each other.

Excrement

All *decaying matter,* which in *decomposing, fertilizes* the Earth.

Social insects: ants, termites, and wasps

Vermin, especially those that carry plagues like rats, fleas, mosquitoes; and those that live in sewers or thrive on filth, like *cockroaches.*

Venereal disease

Activities that must be carried on in the dark, hidden from general knowledge: *Political undergrounds, organized crime, secret police, espionage, plots.*

Cartel or other *secret agreements* between businesses or corporations to fix prices or defraud the public.

Anarchy and anarchists

The *FBI* and *CIA*

Detectives

The totalitarian state

Atomic energy, the atomic bomb, and *bombs* in general

Rape, rapists

Tyrants and dictators

Great wealth, the maximum amount possible: *plutocrats*

Inquisitors, inquisitions; hence, legal torture practiced to extract information as by the Spanish Inquisition, the Gestapo, and the NKVD.

Usury

The *extraction of money under threat of physical violence* as practiced by gangs, mobs, organized criminals.

Terrorists, and *rule by threat or terror*

Race, that is, the *genetic differentiation* of peoples inherited through countless generations—Mongolian, Caucasian, Negro, etc. This must be distinguished sharply from cultural, economic, or class differentiation. The distinction here is factual, like that between male and female. The sex of infants at birth is observed to be male or female by their sex organs. Just so the various races recognize each other by visible differences between them, differences of *genetic* origin.

7

The Houses

Horary astrology is the art of judging circumstances; therefore, the houses, which describe circumstances, are more important in the judgment than the signs. Success depends upon remembering exactly what circumstances and relationships each house controls and always seeking the answer from the viewpoint of that house.

The First House rules the querent and his physical body. In event charts, it rules the person or group initiating the action: that is, whoever makes the first offer or proposition; in games, the home team; the side which fires the first shot in a war chart. In mundane astrology, it rules the people of the nation involved.

The Second House rules the querent's resources, especially his money and income, and his immediate future. In event charts, it rules the resources of whoever initiates the action and his immediate future. In mundane charts, it rules the resources of the nation, the wealth of the people: hence, by analogy, the *Treasury* and the Gross National Product.

The Third House rules the querent's brothers and sisters; his neighbors; the neighborhood he lives in; short journeys; commuting; all the taken-for-granted objects he uses in his daily life; his ability to reason and communicate with others. In an event chart, it rules the same things, but pertaining to the person initiating the action. Here it may also signify rumors or lies, and if very afflicted, it may indicate that he who makes an offer or proposes something is lying. In mundane charts, it rules the nation's newspapers, magazines, telephones, postal service, rumors, elementary schools, and little children.

The Fourth House rules the querent's home, real estate, office, the end of the matter for the querent. In an event chart, it rules the same things for whoever initiated the action. In mundane charts, it rules the land, the people's homes and real estate. Saturn falling in the fourth house of a mundane chart may indicate a housing shortage; Pluto there may indicate vandalism or crime waves affecting property; serious afflictions to the fourth from combinations of Uranus, Neptune, and Jupiter may indicate loss of property through storms, floods, and earthquakes.

The Fifth House rules the querent's children, his love affairs, his gambling and speculation, his hobbies, entertainment of himself and others (parties). It also rules the places he goes to find amusement: parks, resorts, sporting arenas, theatres, gymnasiums, and the games he plays. In event charts, it rules the same things for the person initiating the action. In mundane charts, it rules ambassadors and diplomats from foreign countries; all places of amusement, the public parks, the stock exchanges, the secondary schools, adolescent children, great mansions and estates, palaces, the courts of kings, the theatre and actors.

The Sixth House rules the querent's employment, the general condition of his health, his tenants, employees, and servants. In an event chart, it rules the same things for the person who initiates the action. Thus, in this case, there is an overlapping of values. For instance, in the event that someone offers the querent a job, it is a sixth-house matter for both of them: a job for the querent, an employee for the person who offered it. In mundane charts, the sixth house rules the Civil Service; the Armed Forces; the nation's food reserves, especially grains; places where records are stored, (hence computers); all those who keep the records: librarians, book-keepers, archivists, and so forth. In modern societies, it rules all those who work at routine jobs for wages, whether in offices, factories, or trades. Thus, by analogy, it also rules trade unions, social security programs, unemployment insurance, workmen's compensation, and so forth. It does not, however, rule welfare, because people on welfare live on the charity of the State (twelfth house) and do not work. Therefore the sixth, with its primary meaning of labor, cannot apply to them.

The Seventh House rules the querent's spouse, his business partnerships, his legal contracts, his lawsuits, his astrologer, or any other person who serves him as a counselor or adviser. In classical astrology, this house was called "the enemy of the chart," because malefics here by transit or progression attack the Ascendant, the physical body of the native. In all types of horary work, a heavily afflicted seventh indicates an enemy, an open rupture in a partnership or marriage, or someone who is hiding something from the querent. Saturn here creates a stricture against judgment so that the chart cannot be read.

In event charts, the seventh rules the querent's response to someone else's initial action, proposal, or challenge. In such cases, heavy malefics here may mean that the querent is his own worst enemy or that he acts against his own interests. It also rules the defendant in a lawsuit, the criminal on trial, a condemned person and known criminals who are at large, such as escaped convicts.

In mundane charts, the seventh house rules allies; treaties with other nations; courts of law; public enemies; the public streets and places where people gather, such as town squares; art museums. It also rules public opinion. In war charts, it rules the enemy.

The Eighth House rules the querent's financial obligations, the money owed to others in debts, taxes, or loans. It rules his financial losses and his gains through inheritance; the resources of his spouse and of other people in general. It is a house of peril and may indicate the death of someone inquired about, but never, in a horary chart, the death of the querent himself. It may show that he is in physical peril, especially if the question is about a dangerous undertaking. But however afflicted the eighth house, the astrologer must never forget this basic rule of horary: no chart set up to answer a question ever reveals death of the querent. If the querent were close to death, the chart would have strictures against judgment that would forbid its reading. All *valid* horary charts contain the assumption that the querent will live to see the solution of his problem.

In event charts, the eighth rules the same things for the person initiating the action, but, if the initiator is not the querent, it may show *his* death. Usually in this case, too, strictures will appear in the chart, indicating that the initiator of the action does not live to see the completion of his project. For instance, when John F. Kennedy took his oath of office the first degree of Gemini was rising—an invalid Ascendant. Since all event charts can be read, regardless of strictures, the interpretation here was that he would not finish his term of office, which proved to be true. In events concerning crimes, the eighth rules the detectives. In those concerning murder, it rules the victim.

In mundane charts, it rules the resources of allies; the collection of taxes; the national debt; peril to the people through war, epidemics, natural disasters, famine. In war charts, it rules the resources of the enemy, which include their armaments.

The Ninth House rules the querent's journeys to distant places, especially to foreign countries; his lawyers in a court action; his spouse's brothers and sisters; his religion and church affiliation; his connection with universities and higher education; his grandchildren; foreign associates and business dealings in foreign countries. In event charts, it rules the same things for the person who initiates the action.

In mundane charts, the ninth house rules the Supreme Court; the nation's churches and institutions of higher learning; foreign affairs, foreign trade, international law, world conferences, and world assemblies, such as the United Nations. It also rules the publishing industry and national policy in regard to the dissemination of ideas by any means. Thus, both political propaganda and censorship are shown in this house. In war charts, it rules efforts to blockade the enemy's shores or otherwise cut him off from his sources of supply and trade.

The Tenth House rules the querent's honor, reputation, status, and the worldly position or career that gains these things for him. It is the house of both fame and infamy, for anything that brings notoriety shows here. It also rules the querent's mother, the spouse's real estate, grandchildren's money or resources. An afflicted Saturn here may indicate a decline in prestige, a fall from power, or, in questions about health, a fall that results in broken bones. In questions pertaining to law, it rules the court. In those pertaining to employment, it rules the querent's employer.

In event charts, the tenth house rules these same matters for the person initiating the action.

In mundane charts, the tenth rules the administration of the nation, whether king, president, chancellor, or dictator. It also rules the civil police force and all those who have authority to exert force or pressure upon the citizens. In war charts, it rules the enemy's land and the final outcome of the war for them. If Jupiter transits the tenth house of a national horoscope when a war breaks out, victory is indicated. But if Saturn makes this transit then, the probability of defeat is great. The same holds true for candidates up for election.

The Eleventh House rules the querent's goals, ambitions, friends, adopted children and step-children; also the income he earns from his business or career. It rules his affiliation in groups and clubs; his daughters- and sons-in-law; his mother's money. In event charts, it rules the same matters for the person initiating the action.

In mundane charts, the eleventh house rules the goals of the nation; therefore, the Communist Five Year Plans fall here, as well as national programs to control prices or ration goods, and plans for such things as urban renewal, industrial development, and environmental control. It rules parliaments and legislatures. When afflicted, it indicates that the people are disillusioned.

The Twelfth House rules the querent's past and may indicate family scandals or tragedies before he was born, or skeletons in the family closet. It is the house of involuntary incarceration, therefore, the querent's sojourns in jails or hospitals show here. Very adverse connections between the eighth, the twelfth, and the Ascendant may suggest that the querent is contemplating suicide. This is the house of secret enemies and hidden vices (self-undoing). It rules the spouse's health. In event charts, it rules the same things for the person initiating the action.

In mundane charts, the twelfth house rules the nation's prisons, hospitals, and all those people kept in slavery, peonage, and serfdom. It rules foreign spies (secret enemies) and the activities of organized mobs, such as drug dealing, illicit gambling, and organized prostitution. It rules concentration camps wherever found. In war charts it rules the enemy's espionage, the orphans of war, displaced and homeless people, the wounded, and military hospitals. It is a house of subtle, hidden tyranny.

8

Turning the Radical Chart

When answering questions by the horary method, we are actually dealing with two different levels of reality, which are described simultaneously in the chart constructed for the moment the question is asked. This sounds confusing, but once we understand why it must be so, separating the two levels no longer creates problems.

The chart cast for the moment the question is asked is called the *radical chart*. It is a map of the heavens as seen from a particular place on Earth at that moment. Let us suppose the place is New York City. The radical chart is a picture of the transits over ten or eleven million natal horoscopes of the people who happen to be in New York at that moment. It becomes the natal horoscope of every baby born in New York at that moment. It is the *event chart* for everything begun in New York at that moment: the ship launched, the contract signed, the marriage performed, the convention convened, the murder committed, the case going to trial, the aircraft taking off, the new shop being opened, and so on through a list of the most diverse activities all happening at the same time to different people in New York. Should something of national importance happen then, like the beginning of a dock strike, the outbreak of riots, the nomination of a political candidate, it becomes a *mundane chart*, describing the development and consequences of the action as these concern the nation or the world.

Obviously, a chart can be cast for every moment of every day for every place on Earth. The result of such an effort is meaningless unless we know why the chart was cast and what sort of entity or event it applies to. Is it the birth of a human being, or of a puppy? If both events occurred in the same place at the same time, the charts will be identical, but they cannot be read in the same way because the potential life development of a man is entirely different from the potential life development of a dog. Both man and dog may become famous and be loaded with honors, but never in the same way, for the same reasons. The dog may win all the blue ribbons going and make a fortune for his owners, but he can never become a great concert pianist or win the Nobel Prize for literature. Both man and dog may be abandoned in infancy and subsequently adopted into good homes, but this does not have the same psychological meaning for the dog that it does for the man.

I had a client whose horoscope looked exactly like an earthquake chart. When I told her this, she laughed and said she was born at the height of the most disastrous earthquake suffered by Smyrna, Turkey, in modern times. Her life has resembled a series of earthquakes, being subject—at intervals—to sudden devastation that destroys its stability at the foundations, forcing her to build a new life or career from scratch. But she is a human being; so the earthquakes that shake up her life are always human or social events, not natural disasters. Therefore, the moment of her birth has had an entirely different meaning for her than it did for Smyrna.

These two events, the birth of a human being and the destruction of a city, have different meanings because they happened on different planes of existence, and to different *kinds* of entities. That is why the astrologer must know to what and to whom a chart applies before he can begin to read it.

When you ask a question, the radical chart set up for that moment pertains to everything and anything that may be happening at the same time in your immediate environment. Some of these things may actually be happening to you, but be irrelevant to the question because they are happening on different planes of your complex life, or because they concern entities entirely different from the one in the forefront of your mind—the one which inspired the question. You may ask: "Where did I lose my watch?" At the moment you ask, your wife may be seeking a divorce, your daughter may be having a baby, your son may be going away to school, you may be in danger of losing your job all matters of greater importance than losing your watch. And had you asked about any of these other things instead, the radical chart for the moment would have answered your question. The point is, you didn't ask; therefore, all these more important matters must be ruled out of consideration as irrelevant to the trivial problem of the lost watch. In exactly the same way, *everything* known and unknown that is happening in the larger world around you at that moment is ruled out as irrelevant if it has nothing to do with the lost watch.

The radical chart contains thousands of potential answers to thousands of questions. We are concerned with only one. And even if that one thing is a matter of great importance in your life, it is still a *subordinate circumstance* in your entire life history and development. This must be true because the highest and most complex entity with which astrology can deal is the individual human being. The highest plane of existence with which it can deal is the individual human life. The human being is not a thing, but a mysterious entity and greater than the sum of his or her parts. From time immemorial, among all cultures, this extra something has been called the Soul. In the same way, any human life is greater than the sum of events in that life. We express this by saying, "I did that," "It happened to me," "It was part of my life," or "I felt like that at the time." Thus, we separate our experiences from ourselves so that all of them together never become our whole life history. We even say, "It changed my entire life;" and as we say it, we are admitting that it did not *become* our entire life.

Any question that can be answered by horary astrology concerns a specific detail abstracted from the entire life. Even if the matter is very important to the querent, it is trivial in relation to everything else going on in the world at the same time, which is influenced by the same chart. To point up the special, limited nature of the matter, we turn the radical chart to place the question in the house that rules affairs of that kind. If it is possible, we try to keep the question out of the angles of the radical chart because, regardless of the matter asked about, the first house of the radical chart rules the querent (his whole life and being), and the seventh house rules the astrologer.

Unfortunately, we can't always do this because the first, fourth, seventh, and tenth houses of the radical chart do rule matters of great importance, which clients are bound to ask about at times. For instance, in questions about real estate, the first house rules the buyer, the seventh the seller, the fourth rules the property, and the tenth rules the price. This rulership is invariable, regardless of whether the querent is the buyer or the seller. In questions about litigation or criminal trials, the first house rules the plaintiff, the seventh the defendant, the tenth the court, the fourth the verdict. This rulership is usually invariable; although an innocent querent accused of a crime may be ruled by the first. In these matters the radical chart carries a double meaning and must be read on two levels simultaneously. The astrologer must keep the two levels separate in his mind and not confuse them, which makes such charts harder to read than would be the case otherwise.

In both legal trials and buying and selling real estate, a social framework is involved that goes beyond the querent's immediate concerns. Other people he does not know are affected. There are social implications beyond his control in both cases. For this reason, the radical chart, descriptive of this larger environment, becomes the judgment chart, descriptive of the querent's particular circumstances at the moment. In other words, in these questions, social and personal interests overlap.

When teaching horary astrology, it is common practice for the instructor to announce the time and ask the class to write down the first question that comes to the mind of each student. A chart is constructed for that moment. In this radical chart, which is the same for all the questions, each student, as a querent, is represented by the first house. But, if there are ten students, there will be ten different questions, and each will be placed in a different house of the radical chart. Even if two or more happen to fall in the same house, they will yield different answers if they are from different points of view. If the questions have been exactly phrased and are of real concern to the querents, the master chart will give appropriate answers to all of them. For example:

1. "My sister is planning to sell her house. Will she get the price she is asking?" The querent's sister is ruled by the third. The radical chart is, therefore turned so that the third becomes the Ascendant. Real estate is ruled by the fourth, but, since it is a sister's real estate, this is the fourth from the third (sister), or the sixth. The price of real estate is ruled by the tenth, in this case the tenth from the third (sister), which is the twelfth. The answer will be found, then, in the relationship between the third and the twelfth and their rulers. If this is favorable, the answer will be yes. If unfavorable, it will be no.

2. "Shall I buy a new car at this time or get the old one repaired?" Cars are ruled by the third house. But in this case the chart is not turned because the querent himself must make the decision and take the action necessary to buy a new car. The matter is under his control, while in the previous question it was under a sister's control. The old car already in the querent's possession is ruled by the third house. The new car he may buy is ruled by the third from the third, or the fifth. Which house is in a better condition and in a better relationship to the first (the querent)? If the third is better, he should keep the old car. If the fifth is better, he should get a new one.

3. "My mother has been ill for some time. One doctor advises an operation, another advises against it. Should she have the operation?" The querent's mother is ruled by the tenth house. Therefore, since he is not in control of this situation, the radical chart is turned so that the tenth (mother) becomes the Ascendant. Health is a sixth-house matter, but in this case, since we are considering the *mother's* health, it is the sixth from the tenth, or the third house of the radical chart. If this is favorable, and the rulers of the third and tenth houses are in favorable relation to each other, the operation is indicated. If it is unfavorable, and the relation between the rulers of the tenth and third are so bad as to indicate peril to the life, she should not have the operation. If the matter is indecisive, and indications are not really clear, we may want to go a step further and consider the relative merits of the two doctors. The first one mentioned would be ruled by the third (sixth from tenth); the second one mentioned would be ruled by the sixth from the third or the eighth. If the third house is better than the eighth and its ruler is stronger and better aspected, particularly in relation to the tenth (mother), his advice should be followed. If the eighth is stronger and its ruler is in better relation to the ruler of the tenth, the advice of the second doctor should be followed.

4. "My aunt is dying of cancer. Supposedly I have been mentioned favorably in her will. Will I actually inherit from her? If so, will the amount be large or small?" Once more, we do not turn the chart because the inheritance is (or is not) coming directly to the querent who is the first house of the radical chart. Inheritance is an eighth-house matter; therefore, we place the question there. If it is favorable and its ruler is in favorable relation to the ruler of the first, the querent

will inherit. If an expansive planet (Jupiter or the Sun) is favorably involved, the amount will be large. If Saturn is favorably involved, he will still inherit, but the amount will be disappointing or the estate may be burdened by debts. In questions of this type Neptune must always be considered, because if it is involved among the significators or appears in one of the pertinent houses, it may indicate fraud, deception, or even embezzlement. If Neptune is unfavorably involved, the querent should always be advised to take measures to protect his interests against dishonest trustees or lawyers; or warned that settlement may be held up for years because of lost documents, missing heirs, or the mental condition of an heir. Since inheritance involves many other people and social conditions beyond the querent's control, the outer planets must always be considered with great care before rendering judgment.

5. "My son is the sole heir of a large estate, which has been grossly mismanaged. Will anything be left of it by the time his benefactor dies?" The querent's son is ruled by the fifth house. Therefore, the chart is turned to make this the Ascendant of the judgment chart. His inheritance is ruled by the eighth from the fifth, which is the twelfth of the radical chart. If the twelfth is favorable and its ruler is in good relation to the ruler of the fifth, there will be something left for him. If the relationship is unfavorable and the twelfth is tenanted by afflicted malefic, like Saturn, Mars, or Neptune; or if it suffers bad aspects from such malefics, there will be little, if anything, left for the querent's son.

6. "I am thinking of moving to the suburbs, but to do so would mean going into debt. I would have to buy a more expensive house, a second car, and some new furniture. Is the move wise at this time?" Once more, we do not turn the chart because this matter is completely under the querent's control. The fourth house rules his present home. The seventh (fourth from the fourth) rules the new house and the new situation he would find when he moved. If the fourth is much better than the seventh, he should not move at this time. The debts he could contract by moving would be ruled by the second of the radical chart (the eighth—debt—from the seventh). If this is expansive and favorable, he would have no trouble paying off the debts; if it is badly afflicted, especially by Saturn, he would find himself in an uncomfortable bind and should be advised to wait until he has more money or can make better financial arrangements.

7. "I've been offered a chance to go into business for myself. Shall I take it, with all the risks involved, or shall I stay in my present job, which is very secure and has good prospects for advancement?" Once more, we do not turn the chart because the decision is solely up to the querent. The sixth house of the radical chart rules his present employment, which may, on examination, be less rosy than he thinks. The tenth house rules going into business for himself. If this is better than the sixth and forms better relations to the Ascendant and its ruler, he should go into business for himself. If the sixth is better and forms better relations to the Ascendant, he should stay where he is. The income he might gain from going into business is indicated by the eleventh (second from the tenth). Additional information about his prospects in business can be gained from examining it carefully.

8. "I am thinking of asking Mr. X, another lawyer, to come into partnership with me. Is this wise?" The seventh house of the radical chart rules partnerships and Mr. X, the potential partner. Without any consideration of relations between the seventh and the first, if the seventh is badly afflicted, especially by Saturn, Mars, Neptune, or Uranus, the querent should be advised against the partnership. If the seventh is favorable, relations between it and the first should be examined because, although the partnership might be successful, the querent might not get along well with Mr. X if the two rulers were incompatible, or if either suffered a stressful aspect from Mars (quarrels). Partnerships are so important that, if possible, the querent's natal chart should be examined to determine if it permits him ever to be happy in one or to gain from one.

If this situation were slightly different, so that the question is worded: "At 10:52 a.m. on such-and-such a date, Mr. X offered me a partnership in his law firm. Shall I accept?" the horary becomes an event chart. Mr. X, as the initiator of the action, is ruled by the first house, and the querent, on the receiving end of the proposition (action) is ruled by the seventh.

9. "I am having an affair with a man who is married. He has promised to divorce his wife to marry me. Does he mean it?" The querent's lover is ruled by the fifth house, so the chart is turned to make this the Ascendant. His marriage is ruled by the seventh from the fifth, the eleventh. Evidence that the lover is lying would show as afflictions to the fifth from Mercury (lies), Neptune (deceit and delusions), Saturn (self-interest), or Mars (rash promises). If Uranus (divorce) falls in the eleventh (his marriage), he might get a divorce, but, if the fifth indicated he was lying, he still might not marry the querent. The querent's marriage prospects are indicated by the seventh of the radical chart. If this forms favorable relations with the fifth, which also forms favorable relations with the Ascendant (the querent), but the eleventh is under stress, the lover probably means what he says and is in process of getting a divorce. As in the example above, the astrologer should examine the querent's natal chart because marriage can occur only at times when the natal seventh is strongly affected by solar arc and transit aspects.

In questions like this one, which concern the possibility that someone may be lying, beware of Mercury trine the Moon if either is afflicted by Saturn. No other planetary pattern so strongly indicates a liar.

10. "I have just inherited some money that is invested in municipal bonds. Everyone is urging me to sell the bonds and put the money in the stock market, where it will pay me a better return and be a better hedge against inflation. Should I do this?" Once again we do not turn the chart because bonds are a second house resource, and the decision of what to do with them is solely up to the querent. Stocks are ruled by the fifth (speculation). If the second house is stronger than the fifth and its ruler makes better aspects to the ruler of the first, the querent should keep the bonds and stay out of the stock market. Further testimony may be gained from the eighth (loss). If there are mutual afflictions between the fifth and the eighth, or if an afflicted malefic rules either house or is placed in either, the querent would stand to lose money in the stock market. If the re-

verse is true and the eighth and second mutually afflict each other, the querent would stand to lose money by keeping the bonds.

The astrologer encounters many questions like this, where the relative merits of two houses must be examined in relation to the first house—the querent. It sometimes happens that neither alternative is good. In this case, the querent might lose money both by keeping the bonds and by investing in the stock market. If so, he should be told to look for still another type of investment, and, when he finds it, to ask another question specifically about *that* investment. The astrologer should not suggest a third or fourth alternative on the basis of a chart set up, like this one, to answer an either—or question about two definite alternatives specified in the question. It cannot be stressed too strongly that a horary question covers *only* the matters asked about. If these matters are clouded or unfortunate, the astrologer is never at liberty to suggest something else that had not occurred to the querent. To do so is to assume responsibility for the querent's affairs which is never warranted on the basis of a horary chart. In fact, he should not look for alternatives outside the limits of the question even if the astrologer himself is the querent. Wishful thinking here can lead to many pitfalls through unconsciously extending the scope of the question to matters that were never consciously asked about.

But it is always legitimate to examine the querent's natal horoscope to find a way out. This may reveal that the querent's best investments are in real estate, mortgages, an annuity, or insured bank accounts. The client can then be advised to investigate these fields and to seek advice about any specific one from people qualified to give it.

The astrologer must never forget that he is forbidden by law to practice medicine without a license; to practice law if he is not a member of the bar; or to give financial advice in any but the most general way. We can suggest that a client consult a physician, but we cannot say that he has cancer. We can suggest that he consult a lawyer, but we cannot say that he should sue his neighbor. We can suggest that he should consult a real estate broker but we cannot say that he should buy the vacant lot on the corner.

Certainly we cannot give such advice in answer to a horary question if the client himself does not phrase the question so that a yes or no answer is overwhelmingly clear. Success in horary astrology depends on never forgetting the severe limitations of the horary chart. For any important question there should be at least three clear testimonies of the same answer. If, as in chart 10, Saturn falls in the fifth house, it is a testimony of possible loss. If this Saturn is square Mars, ruler of the second, the loss can be sudden and drastic. If the ruler of the first falls in the fifth, conjunct Saturn, the loss could put the querent in desperate straits. If the first aspect the Moon makes is a conjunction or square to Neptune, the loss will probably occur because the querent will be a victim of fraud. All these indications taken together would make it fairly certain that stocks would be a bad investment for the querent, and he should be so advised.

But are they a bad investment only at this time, or is any speculative investment always dangerous for this querent? Look to the natal horoscope to find out. All things are never possible to all men. This should not be forgotten when doing horary work because the horary chart cannot promise success in a field for which the querent has no aptitude. Again and again you will find that people ask questions about careers or projects for which they have no talent and at which they cannot possibly succeed, although they may have great talent and every possibility of success in some other direction.

Pretty girls with no talent for acting and weak tenth houses will ask when they should try to get on the stage. A barely literate person will ask when his book—sure to be a best seller— will be published. A homosexual will ask when he should marry a certain girl. A person who should never gamble will ask when he can make a killing on the commodity market. Usually the horary chart will answer such questions with an honest negative, or there will be a stricture against judgment forbidding the chart to be read.

There are many times, however, when an impossible question asked in naive faith, yields an ambivalent answer. If so, the astrologer should not argue with the chart or try to force it to give an answer pleasing to himself or the client. In case of an equivocal answer, proceed with caution, for the question may not be quite honest. Remember: there is no *good* time to rob a bank.

9

Timing Events in the Horary Chart

The Moon rules the tide of affairs and how they function. It is also the fastest moving planet in the chart. Therefore, we use it as the horary clock to estimate when a promised event will come to fruition. Cardinal signs and angular houses signify the quickest results. Mutable signs and succedent houses signify the next quickest. Fixed signs and cadent houses signify the slowest. The following table explains this principle.

If the Moon be in:	*The time unit is:*	
Cardinal Sign and Angular House	Shortest	1 Hour
Cardinal Sign and Succedent House	Next Longer	1 Day
Cardinal Sign and Cadent House	Longest	1 Week
Mutable Sign and Angular House	Shortest	1 Day
Mutable Sign and Succedent House	Next Longer	1 Week
Mutable Sign and Cadent House	Longest	1 Month
Fixed Sign and Angular House	Shortest	1 Week
Fixed Sign and Succedent House	Next Longer	1 Month
Fixed Sign and Cadent House	Longest	1 Year

The basic unit selected for the Moon in a cardinal sign and angular house must be reasonable in light of the question and the distance the Moon must travel to form an aspect to one of the significators involved. If the problem is one that must be resolved very quickly, the shortest unit selected might be one minute rather than one hour. Then, all the following units would be speeded up. If the problem is one that will obviously take some time, the shortest unit selected might be one day instead of one hour, which would slow down all the following units.

For example, suppose the question is: "Harry is two hours late for his appointment to sign this important contract. When will we hear from him?" The Moon is in a cardinal sign and a succedent house, and it is six degrees from a conjunction to Mercury (communications). Obviously, since the matter is very important to Harry, he is not going to wait six days to get a message through; unless, of course, he is seriously injured or dead. But the chart does not indicate that. So, to be reasonable, we start with a shorter unit for the Moon in a cardinal sign and an angular house—namely, one minute. Then, the next longer unit for the Moon in a cardinal sign and succedent house, which is the case for this question, would be one hour. So Harry should appear or telephone in six hours.

But suppose the question is: "My lawyer filed the papers for my mother's estate in probate today. When will the estate be settled?" The chart is the same as the one for the previous question: the Moon is in a cardinal sign, a succedent house, and six degrees from a conjunction to Mercury, which is the ruler of the eighth house of inheritance and, therefore, the significator of the estate. Obviously, no probate court is going to settle anything in six days, and it is most unlikely it would settle anything in six weeks. Therefore, to be reasonable, we should stretch the time by two units. If the estate is not complicated, it might be settled in six months. So we assume that the shortest unit (cardinal sign, angular house) would be one week, the next longer would be one month, and the longest one year. If the estate is in a mess or the will contested, settlement might take six years, which would mean we would have to make the shortest unit one month, the next longer one year, and the longest an indefinite time. Such a condition is very rare with the Moon in a cardinal sign.

When it occurs, the delays and complications are clearly shown in the chart by factors other than the Moon. For instance, the ruler of the eighth (inheritance) might form a square to Saturn, (delays and strife) before the Moon could form a conjunction (settlement) to it. Or it might form a prior aspect to Neptune (fraud, embezzlement, missing documents, a missing heir).

Once we have decided on a reasonable time unit, there is a method of checking its reliability. Notice the last planet the Moon passed over in a conjunction, regardless of what sign this planet is in or how far back it is from the present position of the Moon. Something known to the querent happened at that time. The planet the Moon passed over should describe the nature of the event; usually, but not always, the event had some bearing on the question, or it happened to someone connected with the question.

For example, in the question about Harry, who is two hours late for his appointment, the unit of time we selected is an hour. We look to see what planet the Moon last passed over in a conjunction. Suppose this planet is Saturn, which is now 24 degrees behind the Moon. We ask the querent what happened twenty-four hours ago that was even remotely connected with the question. The answer is that some time yesterday, the boss called Harry to remind him to be sure to bring the deeds to the real estate concerned in this deal. This fits, since Saturn rules real estate. But since the Moon's conjunction was formed to Saturn (delays) we may also assume that Harry ran into trouble getting the necessary papers, and this might be the reason why he is late for his appointment.

In the estate matter, we used the same chart, but the time unit selected was one month. That means the Moon passed over Saturn twenty-four *months* ago, and something related to the question should have happened then. What happened two years ago? "That was when Mother first became ill." Saturn: lingering or chronic illness.

If the time unit selected for the Moon's motion is reasonable and seems to be correct, it can be used for all other significators as they form aspects to each other which are important in the outcome. These should be checked to see how many of them become exact at about the same time. In the first question, we decided the querent would hear from Harry in six hours. Harry is ruled by the seventh, since he is the other party signing a contract. Suppose the ruler of the seventh is slightly less than 6 degrees from a trine aspect to the ruler of the fourth (the querent's office), to the fourth cusp, or to a planet in the fourth. It should mean that Harry would appear at the office in slightly *less* than six hours. If the aspect forming is a square, it would mean that he probably couldn't make it in person. If the ruler of the seventh (Harry) forms a favorable aspect in 10 degrees to the ruler of the first (the querent), but an adverse aspect to the fourth in a period of 5½, it should mean that something would happen in 5½ hours to prevent Harry from coming to the office, but that he and the querent will meet in 10 hours somewhere else. If the timing is correct, the querent may say, "The office closes in 5½ hours. If Harry gets here after that, he'll call the boss at home, and we can arrange another place to meet."

Timing the outcome of events is one of the more difficult features of horary astrology. The student should begin to practice it as soon as possible and keep track of when the expected events actually do occur. Generally, you will find that the more deeply the querent is concerned about the matter, the more accurate the timing will be. Often people ask questions out of idle curiosity, as a test of astrology, or simply to needle the astrologer. In such cases, all attempts to time the outcome will fall wide of the mark. Then the querent will think that he has "proved" that astrology doesn't work. Actually, all he will have proved is that he asked a silly question.

10

Placing Events in the Horary Chart

Common questions are those concerning lost objects, strayed animals and children, and people who have disappeared. To find any missing object or person, we look to the house ruling that person or object. We turn the horoscope to make this house the Ascendant of the judgment chart. The ruler of this house becomes the significator of the missing person or thing. Wherever we find that significator is the place or the environment we should search for the missing thing or person.

For instance, "I lost my new literature textbook today. Where did I leave it?" The third house rules books, so it becomes the Ascendant of the judgment chart. Its ruler is Mars, which becomes the significator of the lost book. We find Mars in the third house of the judgment chart (sixth of the radical chart). The book was lost in a third house environment. What are third house environments? Buses, subways, taxis, the immediate neighborhood, and places the querent frequents every day, such as his classrooms. We find the querent does take a bus to school every day, so he might have left it on the bus; except that the Moon, which is not a significator of buses, rules the judgment third. It does, however, rule restaurants and nourishment. Did the querent stop anywhere to eat before going to class? Yes, he stopped at the school cafeteria for a sandwich. Looking further, we find that Venus is in the judgment Ascendant, ruling the book. We conclude that he left the book in the school cafeteria where he goes every day and that it is in the hands of a woman (Venus in the judgment first), probably the cashier, since Venus also rules people who handle money.

In charts of this type, the Moon is always a co-significator of the missing object or person. So we look to the Moon for more details. Here it is in the judgment eleventh (friends), sextile Venus. We conclude a friend found the book, turned it in to the cashier, who is holding it for the querent.

If a chart shows afflictions from Mercury and Saturn to the significator of the lost article, plus definite indications of loss to the querent, the article is probably not lost, but stolen. In thefts perpetrated by drug addicts, Neptune is usually involved. But Neptune may also signify someone who works in the home or office, or someone the querent trusts who is secretly stealing from him. To recover stolen articles, one must find the thief. The question then falls into the missing person category, and it becomes important to know what direction the thief has taken in flight, and what sort of environment he lives in.

The following table gives the bearings by compass of the signs:

Aries—East	Leo—East by North	Sagittarius—East by South
Libra—West	Aquarius—West by North	Gemini—West by South
Cancer—North	Scorpio—North by East	Pisces—North by West
Capricorn—South	Taurus—South by East	Virgo—South by West

If it is known that the article was misplaced in the querent's house or lost on his own property, observe the *element* in which the significator of the lost article falls. Fire signs indicate a place near a wall, a partition, a hearth or other heating element. Air signs indicate a place high up, upper rooms, attics, the tops of high pieces of furniture, places near windows or on stairs. Earth signs indicate places on or near the floor, cellars, gardens, storage bins or pantries. Water signs indicate damp places in the house or grounds, kitchens, bathrooms, sinks, fountains, sewers, wells, and springs.

A mutual reception between the significator of the lost article and the ruler of the house that rules the article, or between either of these and the Moon, indicates that the article is not really lost but has been moved from its customary place to some other, perhaps for safe keeping or temporary convenience. For example, suppose the querent has lost a valuable ring. Venus rules jewelry, and the second house of the radical chart rules the querent's personal property. Gemini falls on the second, therefore, its ruler, Mercury, is significator of his property. Suppose that Mercury is in Libra and Venus is in Virgo. This mutual reception would mean that the ring had been taken from its customary place, probably a jewel box since Gemini rules boxes and Libra rules jewelry, and put into a more utilitarian container (Virgo), perhaps one that had once held cereal or herbs (Virgo). Furthermore, this container had been placed much closer to the floor (Virgo is an Earth sign) than the jewel box had been—possibly in the bottom drawer of a piece of furniture with no legs or very low ones. Then the querent remembers that, before going on her vacation, she put the ring in an empty oatmeal box, along with some valuable coins and a few pieces of antique silver. Then she put the box in the bottom drawer of her desk (Virgo) and covered it with old letters and stationery (Mercury).

In questions about missing animals or people, mutual receptions between the significators mean that the animal or person will be found, but not necessarily in the same condition as when last seen. For instance, suppose the querent asks about his lost dog. The sixth house of the radical chart rules pets. Aries is on the sixth. Mars, its ruler, is in Pisces, the twelfth from the sixth, and Jupiter, ruler of Pisces, is in Aries. Thus, we judge the dog has been taken to a veterinary hospital or to an animal shelter, both ruled by Pisces and the twelfth house. But the querent lives in a city with many veterinary hospitals and several animal shelters. So, in what direction should he look for the one that harbors his dog? Pisces is north by west. He should telephone the suitable places in that direction from his home, and if he knows of one near a body of water (Pisces), he should call it first. In this case, the last planet the Moon passed over was Mars, which indicates that the dog has been in an accident and is probably injured. We know the dog will be found very soon because the Moon is within minutes of a conjunction to Jupiter. Sure enough—before the querent has a chance to call anyone, the veterinarian calls him to say he is holding a dog with a crushed foot (Pisces) and the querent's name and address on his collar. When the querent returns from identifying his dog and arranging for an operation on its foot, he says that the vet's hospital was not near any water, but it was next door to a shop that sold tropical fish!

Directions may also be found by houses. In the first quadrant of the chart, the direction changes from due east to due north; in the second quadrant from due north to due west; in the third quadrant from due west to due south; in the last quadrant from due south to due east. As follows:

First—East	Fourth—North	Seventh—West	10th—South
Second—N by E	Fifth—N by W	Eighth—W by S	Eleventh—E by S
Third—Northeast	Sixth—W by NW	Ninth—Southwest	12th—E by SE

By combining the direction of the signs with those of the houses, a location can be found quite exactly. For instance, if Aries falls on the eleventh house and the significator of the object sought is there, the direction would veer more to the east than to the south. This might mean that given the choice of several dwellings, we would select the one farthest to the east. If an object is sought in a particular house and its significator is in Aries, it would be found near a wall. With Aries on the eleventh, we would look for a southeast corner, and search the eastern side.

Directions may also become important when one is trying to choose a site on which to build, or trying to decide which of several houses in a subdivision to buy. The sign or angle containing a benefic, or the one whose significator is most favorably aspected by benefics should be chosen. Those containing malefics should be avoided.

Missing people have often traveled to another town or city. If the significator of the missing person falls in Sagittarius or in the ninth house, he should be sought in a foreign country. If it falls in Gemini or in the third house, he is in the neighborhood or in an environment familiar to him. But in a chart cast for the attempt to assassinate Governor Wallace, the significator of the assassin (Neptune) fell in Sagittarius in the third house. The reading was that he was in an environment familiar to him (a shopping center) but he was a long way from home, a stranger to that specific place.

11

The Aspects

In horary astrology, the houses, which describe circumstances, are more important than the signs, which describe character. By the same reasoning, aspects, which describe how circumstances will operate, are more important than the planets, whose primary uses in this branch of astrology are as significators of things, people, or conditions.

Saturn and Mars are malefics, but if either forms a favorable aspect to the significator of the question, a person, thing, or circumstance described by Saturn or Mars will aid in bringing a favorable outcome. Jupiter and Venus are benefics, but if either forms an unfavorable aspect to a significator, a person, thing or circumstance described by Jupiter or Venus will hinder a favorable outcome. This means that good aspects bring out the favorable side of malefics while bad aspects increase their malevolence. And bad aspects bring out the unfavorable side of benefics while good aspects increase their benevolence. When the outcome of a matter depends upon Saturn, however favorable it seems, it may be delayed because it is the nature of Saturn to slow everything down. If the outcome depends upon Mars, it may be hastened because it is the nature of Mars to act precipitously, even rashly.

In horary astrology, the Sun is regarded as a benefic. Mercury and the Moon are considered to be neutral. Uranus, Neptune, and Pluto generally indicate people or circumstances beyond the querent's control. They describe social conditions or situations that the querent cannot influence or change, factors that may be unknown to him. When they form strong adverse aspects to the significators of the question, social conditions beyond the querent's control hinder the outcome in an almost fatalistic way. If the adverse aspects involve Saturn, Mars, and either the Sun or the Moon, the chart may take on a truly malignant cast. These conditions appear in charts set up to find a missing person when the person sought is dead; in charts asking about the wisdom of forming some association with another person when that person is a criminal; or in charts asking about some project that would expose the querent to extreme danger or disgrace.

In mundane charts or those set up to judge an event, Uranus, Neptune, and Pluto should be used as the rulers of Aquarius, Pisces, and Scorpio because both mundane and personal events always have social ramifications beyond the querent's control. But in charts set up to answer a simple question, Saturn, Jupiter, and Mars seem to work better as the rulers of those signs, reserving the three outer planets to describe any factors that exist outside the scope of the question in society, but which may still influence the outcome if the querent can recognize them and adapt to them.

If favorably aspected, the three outer planets may help to bring a favorable outcome through unexpected, lucky breaks or through the exposure of something unknown. If Uranus is well aspected, it may bring great benefits through a disaster or holocaust; Neptune well-aspected may bring glamour, fame, or money, but the benefits are ephemeral and the money is like fairy gold, which one can seldom keep. Pluto well-aspected brings benefits through the discovery of something unknown or through the exposure of criminal activity that was injuring the querent. Pluto becomes important in questions about missing heirs, unknown inheritances, people who have been kidnaped, and whether a particular person is alive or dead.

In horary charts we always use the Moon's Nodes. They are points of fatality, and any planet, whether a significator in the question or not, that falls in the degree of the Nodes, no matter what sign it is in, gives an added depth and importance to the chart.

In horoscopes set up to answer questions, we use only the classical Ptolemaic aspects. The trine, sextile, conjunction, parallel, and mutual reception between the significators indicate a favorable outcome unless the significators are so weak or afflicted by other planets that they are almost powerless. In such cases, the outcome may still be affirmative, but it may be spoiled in some way, or it may turn out to be something the querent finds he doesn't want after all.

The square, opposition, and contraparallel between the significators generally deny a favorable outcome.

The semisextile, septile, quintile, biquintile, semisquare, and sesquiquadrate are not used in horary astrology. If they occur between significators, they may bring minor help or interference, but they are not strong enough to affect the final outcome. Therefore, consideration of them merely clutters the chart and hinders the astrologer's clarity of judgment.

The quincunx, or inconjunct, is in a category by itself. In mundane charts it has great importance if it occurs between malefics, between a malefic and one of the significators, or between a malefic and the Ascendant. It must also be carefully considered in the judgment of events. The quincunx might be called "the Uranian aspect," because its action is sudden, unpredictable, violent, or fateful. It is either a sixth-house or an eighth-house aspect—that is, planets in quincunx to each other are either six or eight houses apart. Therefore, it has a connotation of illness or death. In mundane charts set up for the moment a war breaks out or an assassination occurs, quincunxes abound with orbs of 30 minutes or less. You will also find them in charts set up to locate missing persons or animals if the person or animal will be found dead or badly injured.

In setting up election charts for airplane flights, dangerous voyages, or explorations, long automobile trips, or surgery, quincunxes should be avoided. Squares or oppositions indicate difficulties, conflicts, discomfort, or serious hindrances, but unless quincunxes appear they do not indicate the probability of death or permanent injury to the health.

In horary astrology, only applying aspects are considered when predicting the outcome of events or of the question. Past aspects describe conditions that prevailed (or may still prevail) prior to the occurrence of the event or to asking the question. An applying aspect is one where the faster planet is moving toward a slower planet. When all the planets are moving at their average rate, their order, from the fastest to the slowest, is as follows: Moon, Mercury, Venus, Sun, Mars, Jupiter, Saturn, Uranus, Neptune, and Pluto. Generally, this order is reliable, but there are times when the phenomenon of retrogradation disturbs it. The Sun and Moon are never retrograde; they maintain their average daily motions of about one degree for the Sun and about twelve for the Moon throughout the year, with only slight variation. All the other planets are retrograde at times. When a planet is changing from direct to retrograde motion or vice versa, it is said to be *stationary,* because it appears to be standing still in the heavens from the point of view of an observer on Earth. The influence of a stationary planet is extremely powerful; and, during the period of its station, all the other planets may be moving faster and therefore applying to it.

Mercury is retrograde three times a year; therefore, it makes six stations. Venus retrogrades twice every three years. Mars retrogrades once every other year. All the other planets retrograde once each year. Except for Mercury and Venus, the planets turn retrograde when the Sun begins to approach an opposition to them, and they turn direct when the opposition is pulling away. Jupiter changes direction when it is trine the Sun, the others when they are square the Sun.

Mercury can never be more than 28 degrees from the Sun. It forms a station and turns retrograde when it reaches its maximum distance ahead of the Sun. It forms another station and turns direct when it reaches its maximum distance behind the Sun. At these times any planet, even Pluto, may be moving faster than Mercury and therefore applying to it. Mercury moves at its fastest rate when conjunct the Sun. It is then said to be *combust*, a condition which is considered to be unfavorable.

Venus can never be more than 46 degrees from the Sun. It turns retrograde at maximum distance ahead of the Sun and turns direct the same distance behind the Sun. It also moves at its greatest speed when conjunct the Sun, but the combust condition is not considered to be as unfavorable for Venus as for Mercury. The other planets move at their maximum *direct* speed when conjunct the Sun and at their maximum *retrograde* speed when in opposition to it.

When the planets beyond the Earth's orbit are conjunction the Sun, they are said to be *under the Sun's rays*. While this condition will not necessarily deny a favorable outcome to the question, the planet's freedom of action is inhibited. Its power to influence earthly affairs is lessened because when it is under the Sun's rays, it cannot be seen at any time from any place on Earth. It is as if, from our point of view, that planet temporarily ceased to exist, blotted out by the Sun. The ancients set great store by this and considered it evil. Modem astrologers pay less attention to it.

Pluto needs special consideration because of its extraordinary orbit. This is an extreme ellipse. At times Pluto's distance north or south of the celestial equator is greater than that of any other planet, even the Moon. This means its parallels to other planets may be formed at quite different times from its aspects to the same planets in longitude. It also has a greater inclination to the ecliptic than any other planet. Because of these factors, its motion through the signs varies greatly. When it is farthest from the Sun (aphelion) in the signs Aries, Taurus, and Gemini, its motion is very slow. When it is closest to the Sun (perihelion) in the signs Libra, Scorpio, and Sagittarius, its motion is comparatively fast. Toward the end of the sign Virgo, it begins to move faster than Neptune and crosses Neptune's orbit. It remains inside Neptune's orbit until it approaches the end of Sagittarius, when it slows down, crosses Neptune's orbit again, and once more moves out beyond it. During this period, Pluto is closer to the Earth than Neptune, and its influence upon earthly affairs should be most conspicuous then.

We have recently entered this period of Pluto's rapid motion. It is beginning to seem that all our most grievous social problems are indeed Plutonian. It rules the atomic bomb, total war, massive corruption in government, repressive dictatorships, organized crime, juvenile delinquency, racial strife, sexual violence (sadism, rape, and sex-murders), gangsterism, and genocide. I believe that Pluto is a comet recently captured by our solar system. It is small, so that the gravitational pull of other planets upon it could have a marked influence upon its orbit, which would eventually straighten it out, pulling it closer to the ecliptic and making its motion through the signs more regular. Pluto was discovered in 1930, when it crossed the ecliptic in the middle of Cancer. Therefore, we have been able to observe it for less than one quarter of its total orbit. During all this time it has been picking up speed. The assumption that this acceleration will decrease is a theoretical one. If future observation proves it to be false, Pluto will never again move outside Neptune's orbit. Such an unusual cosmic event would have important consequences upon astrological theory and might make it necessary for us to reexamine some of our ideas.

12

Further Considerations that Affect Judgment

1. *The Moon's Nodes.* The Nodes of any planet are the two points in space where it crosses the plane of the ecliptic. Most planetary Nodes move very slowly and they are not considered important in horary astrology. But the Moon's Nodes move backward at the average rate of three minutes per day, and complete a cycle in about eighteen and one-half years. They are sensitive points in any horoscope because they mark the area of solar and lunar eclipses. When the Sun and Moon are in conjunction within ten degrees of the Moon's Nodes, it means that the Earth, Sun, and Moon are all lined up in the same plane. The Moon will pass between the Earth and the Sun, temporarily eclipsing its light. When the Sun and Moon are in opposition within ten degrees of the Moon's Nodes, the Earth will lie between the Sun and Moon. Its shadow will fall across the face of the full Moon, eclipsing its light. The closer the Moon and Sun are to the degree of the Nodes, the longer the eclipse will last and the closer it will approach totality.

Eclipses are extremely important in all horary and mundane work, where they have a connotation of the sudden outbreak of violence. Earthquakes, volcanic eruptions, the onset of wars and riots, the death of public men, the assassination of national leaders, sudden economic or political changes are all estimated to occur when heavy planets or Mars form exact squares or conjunctions to the degree of an eclipse that was visible in the nation concerned or fell upon a sensitive degree of the national chart.

Since eclipses can never occur except close to the degree of the Moon's Nodes, these points are sensitive degrees in any chart. In horary astrology, any planet falling in the exact degree of the Nodes, *regardless of what sign it is in,* is a *fateful* testimony. The Nodes are sometimes regarded as Karmic points that act like an adverse combination of Saturn and Uranus to bring sudden retribution or calamity to someone concerned with the outcome of the question or event. When malefics form quincunxes to the lights and Ascendant and a malefic is also in the degree of the Nodes, the pattern may indicate the death of someone vital to the outcome—a sudden, accidental death that makes no sense in any rational context of interpretation.

If the chart permits, a well-aspected benefic may bring sudden fame or fortune in a fateful manner if in the same degree as the Nodes. As with favorable aspects to Uranus, however, the benefit may come through the death or misfortune of someone else.

2. *Eclipses.* If a question is asked or an event occurs on the day of an eclipse of the Sun, the matter will have to be revised in some important way or circumstances beyond the control of the querent will cause it to collapse. If an eclipse of the Moon follows in two weeks, the revision will have to be made then, and the affair will not prosper even with the revision. If the time unit permits, the final collapse usually comes when Mars crosses the eclipse point in a hard aspect. An example of how this works was the Democratic Convention of 1972, which opened on the day of an eclipse of the Sun. Two weeks later, when the Moon was eclipsed, the vice-presidential candidate selected by the Convention was ditched, and a new vice-presidential candidate was selected. The campaign did not prosper, even after this revision. Mars made the square aspect to the eclipse point at the end of October 1972.

3. *Besiegement.* When the Moon has passed a conjunction to a malefic and the next aspect it forms is a conjunction to another malefic, it is said to be besieged. Regardless of how favorable other indicators may be, this condition of the Moon denies a favorable outcome. The ancient astrologers considered that the Moon was besieged only when it formed conjunction or opposition aspects to the two malefics, but many modern astrologers read this condition to prevail in squares as well. For example, if the Moon has just passed a conjunction to Saturn and the next aspect it forms is a square to another malefic, or if it has just passed a square to Saturn and the next aspect it forms is a square to Mars, it is said to be besieged. This gives a wider scope to the condition, but the situation is so unfavorable that I think modern astrologers are justified in reading it as denial of a favorable outcome.

4. *Impedition.* When a planet is moving into an aspect with another planet, but the second planet will leave the sign it is in before the aspect can be formed, or if the applying planet turns retrograde before the aspect can be formed, the aspect is said to be *impedited.* This ancient term survives in modern English in the noun *impediment,* which means blockage or interference. For example, the Moon is 25 Cancer about to form a trine to the Sun at 28 Scorpio. The time unit for this aspect to form is three weeks. The Sun moves into Sagittarius in two days,

however. Therefore, the aspect cannot be formed, and if the Moon at 25 Cancer has no other aspect than this to form before it leaves the sign, it must be considered void-of-course and the chart unfit for judgment.

Another example: Mercury is applying to a square to Saturn, but before it can form the aspect, it turns retrograde. The evil promised by the square will not come about. Rather, the matter will be held in abeyance and a period of frustration will occur while Mercury is retrograde and the whole project may be discarded. If it survives until Mercury turns direct, it will undoubtedly have undergone so much revision that the original question no longer applies. If it is still pertinent, however, a square between Mercury and Saturn does not necessarily deny a favorable outcome if Mercury makes favorable aspects to other planets before it can form the square. For instance, if Mercury retrogrades back and forth over a trine to Jupiter, the square it was about to form to Saturn may only mean that someone involved is a crook or a liar, but that his dishonesty cannot prevail, however inconvenient or costly it may be.

Thus, impedition can spoil what looks like a favorable outcome on the surface, or it can help to prevent an unfavorable outcome.

5. *Translation of Light.* The Moon functions through its aspects with other planets. In itself it is neutral. It takes on the coloration and influence of the planets it aspects and translates these influences into activity which helps or hinders the matter. In horary astrology, the Moon functions only in the sign it is in when the question was asked or the event occurred. That is why, when the Moon makes no major aspect to any planet before it leaves the sign (void-of-course), all activity the querent may generate proves pointless. None of the planets, however favorable their relations to each other, can influence the matter without the intercession of the Moon.

The Moon must be applying to some other planet in a major aspect and it must make this aspect exactly before it leaves the sign it is in for a horary chart to be valid and readable,. However, it may have made one, two, or many aspects from this sign before the question was asked or the event occurred. All these past aspects should have some bearing on the status of the problem. They should describe past events leading up to it or people concerned with it. Such events may or may not be known to the querent, but they are important to him because their influence contributed to the creation of some facet of the problem or may have set up conditions in the past which will lead to a favorable outcome.

As the Moon moves rapidly from one aspect to the next, we say it *carries the light* or *translates the light* from one planet to the next. The more aspects the Moon has formed before the question was asked, the more complex it is and the more it has been shaped by past conditions. If the Moon has made only one or two aspects before the question was asked, but has numerous aspects yet to form before it leaves the sign, the complexity lies in the future. Many things will happen before the matter is brought to a conclusion.

To see how this works, let us open an ephemeris anywhere and look at any day—October 26, 1972, for example. We see that at 7:00 a.m. EST, the Moon is at 28 Gemini 20. All the possible aspects it could make in Gemini have been formed. It is void of course, therefore, until it enters Cancer at 9:46 a.m. After entering Cancer, the Moon makes a square to Pluto at 2:54 p.m., a trine to the Sun at 3:40 p.m., and an opposition to Jupiter at 4:36 p.m. On the following day, it makes a contraparallel to Jupiter at 7:25 a.m., a square to Mars at 3:20 p.m., a square to Uranus at 7:13 p.m., a contraparallel to Mercury at 9:10 p.m., and a contraparallel to Saturn at 11:39 p.m. On the 28th, it makes a trine to Mercury at 8:17 a.m. and a sextile to Venus at the same moment. After that it makes no further aspects until it enters Leo at 1:16 p.m.

This is an unusually active Moon on which a great many questions could be resolved for better or worse. From 2:54 p.m. on the 26th, when it picked up its first influence (adverse) from the square to Pluto until 8:17 a.m. on the 28th, when it makes its last aspects (favorable) to Mercury and Venus, the Moon translates the light from Pluto to the Sun, to Neptune, to Jupiter, to Mars, to Uranus, to Mercury, to Saturn, and finally dumps all these influences onto Mercury and Venus at the same moment in the highly favorable trine and sextile.

Now, if a question is asked on the 26th between 2:54 p.m., when the Moon squared Pluto and 3.40 p.m., when it will trine the Sun, the reading would be that a troublesome person or an unfortunate event represented by Pluto would be favorably resolved through the agency of the Sun. If a question is asked between 3:20 p.m. and 7:13 p.m. on the 27th, the Moon would be passing from a square to Mars to a square to Uranus. It would be besieged. The reading would be one of disaster or serious misfortune because all the previous influences would be transferred to violent Mars before being passed on to violent and unpredictable Uranus. The situation would be especially dangerous because when the Moon squares Mars, it is crossing from 18 to 19 Cancer, the degree of the eclipse of the Sun on July 10, 1972. It therefore carries the light not only from Mars to Uranus, but also from the eclipse, now activated by Mars to Uranus. The matter asked about might well be interfered with or completely shoved aside by a public disaster involving violence, such as an attempted assassination of a public figure or an attack upon someone involved in the question. This would be particularly true if the matter inquired about had its inception on the day of the eclipse.

But if a question is asked between 11:39 p.m. on the 27th and 8:17 a.m. on the 28th, all the previous adverse influences would be speedily resolved through the benefic agency of Mercury and Venus acting together. The reading would then be that the querent had passed through an exceedingly trying time that might even have endangered his life at one point. But now, partly because of all he had learned from these trying experiences, he is finally about to get a break: the quarrels would be amicably settled, he would win his suit, the lost papers would be found, the patient would live, he would recover the stolen goods or be paid for them, he would get the job he had long sought or something better. The only flaw would be that whoever or whatever had died during the Moon's besiegement on the degree of the eclipse could not be brought back to life.

6. *Retrograde Planets.* Retrogradation lessens the power of a planet for constructive or beneficial action. When retrograde, a planet becomes a passive, rather than an active, force. It becomes a victim of circumstance, rather than an initiator of events. Judgment about the things ruled by the planet is poor. Frequently the querent is misinformed or not informed at all about matters the planet rules. The course of events becomes abnormal, beset by difficulties, and if the whole matter does not collapse, the querent is led into a blind alley or into a frustrated bind where he can neither go forward nor backward. To start a project when its planetary ruler is retrograde usually proves to be costly and should be avoided. If one or more of the significators in a question are retrograde, the querent should be advised to wait, if possible, until they turn direct before going ahead with his plans.

A retrograde Mercury affects the whole chart. It means that someone concerned with the affair will change his mind, causing the matter to collapse or to be drastically revised. Often it is the querent who changes his mind and no longer wants the thing he asked about after Mercury turns direct. Ideas that seem brilliant while Mercury is retrograde show serious flaws after it turns direct. Mercury retrograde interferes with communication and causes people to misunderstand each other for foolish reasons. The querent should be advised not to start any new project or to begin any important activity when Mercury is retrograde—no matter how attractive the rest of the chart seems.

In the most general sense, Mars rules activity and the initiation of action. For some strange reason, most people feel almost uncontrollable urges to start important ventures when Mars is retrograde. Since all action is delayed then, or hampered, tempers grow short, people become impatient, resentments deepen, acrimonious arguments aggravate dissension, and suppressed ill feelings come to the surface. Ventures begun impatiently under such a load of animosity are usually misguided and will end in the defeat or confusion of the querent. Nothing is accomplished by activity under a retrograde Mars. But since it retrogrades for several months every other year, it is not always possible to avoid starting things. The querent should be warned, however, not to:

Buy a car. It will be accident prone and he may be seriously hurt. If he can't struggle along with the old one until Mars turns direct, he should rent one for the duration.

Undergo surgery unless it is absolutely unavoidable, as would be the case if he broke a bone or was in an accident.

Have sexual intercourse for the first time with a woman he loves. The affair will end badly in mutual hatred or with serious injury to one or both people. Marriages planned to occur with Mars retrograde should be postponed.

Start a lawsuit. He who does will lose his case.

Start a new job. His best efforts will not please his boss.

Begin a long or dangerous journey.

Hire a new employee, sign a contract, arrange a partnership, move into a new house, or take title to property. The result would be animosity, loss, or physical danger to the querent.

In mundane astrology, if Mars is retrograde:

When a treaty is signed, it will be abrogated.

When a ruler or elected official comes to power or assumes office, his administration will be unfortunate, plagued by defeats, attrition of power, misunderstandings, and ill will. He may be disgraced, impeached, or killed in office.

When a nation takes aggressive action against another to start a war or a campaign, the aggressor will be defeated with great loss of life, material, and prestige. The Arabs closed the Port of Eilat and started the Six Day War with Israel on a retrograde Mars. President Johnson began the bombing of North Vietnam on a retrograde Mars. Hitler invaded Russia on a retrograde Mercury and was then trapped by the Russian winter when Mars turned retrograde on September 7. In 1933, Mars was retrograde from January 21 to April 12. Hitler came to power on January 30. He instigated a policy of aggressive war to conquer all Europe, and was eventually defeated. Franklin Roosevelt was inaugurated on March 4, when the economy of the country had collapsed. During his administration, an assassin attempted to shoot him, a foreign power attacked American territory, and he died in office before seeing the end of the war. It is interesting that these two men assumed power within weeks of each other and died within weeks of each other.

McKinley was inaugurated March 4, 1901. He was assassinated. John Kennedy was inaugurated on January 20, 1961. He was assassinated. Lincoln was reelected in November 1864. He was assassinated. Mars was retrograde on all these occasions.

When judging charts for the outbreak of war, remember it is the aggressor nation that suffers from the retrograde Mars. However remote and impossible victory may seem to be for the defenders, it will be theirs.

Retrogradation of the other planets is not so serious, but the querent should not start ventures they rule at such times, and in the horary judgment, ventures they rule will be hampered or come to nothing.

When Venus is retrograde, large social affairs go badly, attempts to raise money are disappointing, and attempts to conciliate others come to nothing. In mundane affairs, treaty negotiations break down or treaties signed then are betrayed. Serious epidemics, like those of influenza and typhus of 1918, often begin when Venus is retrograde.

When Jupiter is retrograde, people should not try to increase their power or popularity. A retrograde Jupiter promises much and delivers little but disappointment. Candidates who are nominated or decide to run for election when Jupiter is retrograde usually suffer defeat or, if elected, suffer loss of power and prestige. In 1972, both McGovern and Nixon were nominated on Jupiter retrograde, with Neptune also retrograde in McGovern's case.

A retrograde Saturn is an indication of delay in any venture.

It is the significator of a person who cannot be trusted or of something irrevocably lost. If it signifies a missing person or animal, they may be found dead if the Saturn is otherwise afflicted.

When Uranus, Neptune, and Pluto are retrograde, their power to do subtle, undercover damage is increased. But the harm they have done will not come into the open until they turn direct.

7. Exaltation and Debility. One of the traditional teachings of astrology that is sometimes important in horary judgments is that planets are strongest when placed in the signs they rule or in the signs of their exaltation; and that they are weakest when placed in their detriments or fall. The detriment of a planet is the sign opposite one it rules. The fall is the sign opposite its exaltation. These positions are as follows:

Planet	*Rules*	*Detriment*	*Exaltation*	*Fall*
Sun	Leo	Aquarius	Aries	Libra
Moon	Cancer	Capricorn	Taurus	Scorpio
Mercury	Gemini-Virgo	Sagittarius	Virgo	Pisces
Venus	Libra-Taurus	Aries-Scorpio	Pisces	Virgo
Mars	Aries-Scorpio	Libra-Taurus	Capricorn	Cancer
Saturn	Capricorn-Aquarius	Cancer-Leo	Libra	Aries
Jupiter	Sagittarius-Pisces	Gemini-Virgo	Cancer	Capricorn

Signs of exaltation and fall have not yet been agreed upon for the outer planets. We have not known of them long enough to observe with assurance in which signs they may be strongest. There is, however, a growing consensus that Neptune, as ruler of Pisces, may be strongly placed in Cancer and rather unfortunate in Capricorn. There seems to be no doubt any longer that it does rule Pisces and is badly placed in Virgo. Uranus is so strongly placed in Scorpio that this has been called a position of genius. It is peculiarly violent and socially disruptive in Leo, certainly its detriment. Since we have not yet observed a full revolution of Pluto, it is impossible to say what its exaltation and fall may be.

In any case, exaltations and debilities of the outer planets can hardly have much bearing on horary judgments because of the length of time they stay in each sign. This may be another good reason for using the old rulerships. On the other hand, if a question is asked at a time when one of the outer planets is about to change signs, the very slowness of movement makes the change highly significant. If the outcome of the question depends upon any sort of social cooperation (as would be the case in questions about employment, investments, careers, foreign travel), and Uranus, Neptune, or Pluto will change signs before the matter can be settled, the movement and meaning of the signs involved should be carefully considered. The judgment should include the caution that social conditions over which the querent has no control are about to change, and that this change will affect the outcome. The, the effect may be either favorable or unfavorable, depending upon aspects. Either way, the querent will not be able to control or do much about it.

For example, in 1972, Pluto was changing from Virgo into Libra. One mundane event that coincided with this planetary movement has been a winding down of the war in Indo-China. If the querent was seeking employment that depended upon the war, his services would not be needed when the war ended. But no matter how much he needed the job, or what his qualifications were, he could do nothing to influence the social conditions that dictated peace. Another mundane event coinciding with Pluto's movement was the opening of trade between the U.S. and China and Russia. A querent interested in importing and exporting goods, or in financing such ventures, might gain greatly from the change, but he himself would be powerless to bring the change about.

In mundane astrology, these sign changes of the slow planets are of the utmost importance because they mark the end of eras of political power, of peace or war, of fashionable ideologies, or long prevailing economic conditions. They always mark a change in public opinion which shows up quickly in fashions in clothes, art, literature, motion pictures, voting trends, and ideas about religion, politics, and society. The mundane astrologer should study the history of the world since the end of the eighteenth century, when Uranus was discovered. He should consider the sudden economic, political, and technological changes that coincided with these movements. In many cases such changes will affect the outcome of a question in a fateful way. Such changes can be important in judging the outcome of elections, the rise to power of certain world figures, and the removal of others from the scene. It is important to remember that the more mundane power a man attains the less individual freedom he has. Successful politicians and popular or glamorous people are always in tune with their times. They are successful because public opinion agrees with them at certain times. When public opinion changes but they do not, they are discarded. And when the heavy planets move into new signs, public opinion does change, sometimes radically, almost overnight.

8. Fixed Stars. A few stars with northern latitude, or with declination, if south, that is on or close to the ecliptic, are considered important in horary and mundane astrology. These stars operate only when conjunction or opposition a planet, the MC, or the Ascendant. The orb allowed is one degree, and the aspect may be figured in either longitude or right ascension.

A list of these stars, with their effect and approximate position in longitude, follows.

Algol, a variable binary, at 25 Taurus 30, is considered the most malevolent of stars; it is associated with accidents to the throat and neck and with death by hanging, beheading, strangulation, or wounds of the throat and neck. Mars, Saturn, Uranus, or the Sun, if afflicted on this degree, may indicate violence or great physical danger in the horary chart. Algol is often stressed in criminal maps and in questions about murder. If prominent and afflicted in mundane charts, it may presage great disasters such as fires, earthquakes, mine cave-ins, where many people die of suffocation.

Alcyone, the largest of the Pleiades, at 29 Taurus, is called the Weeping Sister, a star of sorrow. Ptolemy said it has the nature of the Moon afflicted by Mars.

Aldebaran, a first magnitude star at 8 Gemini 50, is of the nature of Mars, it is a star of war and violence, fortunate if well aspected in the charts of military leaders. It is in conjunction with Uranus and rising in the July 4, 1776, map of the United States.

Castor, a second magnitude star at 19 Cancer 30, is associated with crippling of the limbs if on the Ascendant, MC, ruler, Moon, or Sun and any of these points are badly afflicted, especially by Saturn, Uranus, and Neptune. It is often found prominently placed and afflicted in charts of the mentally ill.

North and South Asellus, a pair of dim stars with latitude on the equatorial plane, at 6 Leo 30 and 7 Leo 40 respectively. If rising afflicted and the lights are also afflicted, they are indicators of blindness. No operation on the eyes should ever be performed when any planet is conjunct or opposing these stars.

Regulus, a first magnitude star at 29 Leo, is of the nature of Mars conjunct Jupiter. It is the star of kings and important in mundane work. If rising or conjunct the MC and Jupiter or the Sun, it may bring an unknown or otherwise seemingly ordinary person to high office and great power. Lyndon B. Johnson had this configuration. If afflicted, it may still bring power, but the career may end suddenly in disgrace, deposition, or violent death.

Vindemiatrix, a bright star at 8 Libra 50, is called the Star of Widowhood. It is especially fateful when conjunct the Moon's Nodes. It is also a star of martyrdom and is often found prominent in the charts of mystics and those interested in the occult. Gandhi had the Sun on this star. No marriage chart should ever be set up for a time when any planet, the Nodes, the MC, or Ascendant is conjunct or in opposition to Vindemiatrix.

Spica and *Arcturus,* two first magnitude stars at 23 Libra. Spica has been called the only wholly benefic fixed star, but it is impossible to separate its influence from that of Arcturus, which has a nature like that of Aldebaran and Regulus combined, and may lead to sudden downfall or disgrace. In a war chart, if prominent and well aspected, these stars indicate victory.

The North Scale, a second magnitude star at 18 Scorpio 30, has been called "the accursed degree of the accursed sign" since ancient times, but probably not because of the presence of this star, which was not in this position in ancient times. The star is actually considered rather fortunate, especially in its effect on the intelligence, which is often brilliant. In horary and mundane work, the unfortunate nature of the degree seems to transcend the influence of the star. A malefic here is an indicator of tragedy. Robert Kennedy had Saturn here.

Antares, a red giant at 8 Sagittarius 30 and opposing Aldebaran, acts like a Mars-Jupiter conjunction. It is associated with war. If well configured with significators of employment or the career, the native may attain great prominence through war. If badly configured with malefics, war may bring him loss, death, or disgrace. Winston Churchill had the Sun on Antares. Afflictions here may indicate blindness if other testimonies concur. This star is on the descendant of the United States horoscope.

Aculeus and *Acumen,* two star clusters at 25 and 28 Sagittarius, respectively, are of the nature of Mars afflicting the Moon and are indicators of blindness. As with the area 6-7 Leo, no surgery that might affect the eyes should be planned when any planet or personal point is near these degrees.

Facies, a star cluster at 7 Capricorn 30, is another area of blindness.

Vega, a first magnitude star at 14 Capricorn 30, has a benefic influence associated with politics and politicians. If well-aspected, it helps to confer wealth upon those dealing with governments. In mundane charts, it is an indication of victory in war. It is now in the latitude of Washington, D.C. and circling the MC there.

Fomalhaut, a first magnitude star at 3 Pisces, is an indicator of congenital birth defects or inherited illness when on any personal point and afflicted by malefics it. Saturn was here, afflicted by Pluto and Uranus when the thalidomide babies were conceived. Fomalhaut is a Karmic star with a profound occult significance. For centuries, it was associated with magic and alchemy. If angular, conjunct the Sun, Moon, or Jupiter, and these are well aspected by Pluto, Neptune, or Uranus, it is said to indicate a person whose Karmic destiny is occult mastery. It brings fame through the occult. If this fame is exploited for material ends, however, the result may be unfortunate.

Markab, a second magnitude star at 23 Pisces, is another Karmic star of great sorrow and tragedy that comes to the native through no fault or action of his own. If conjunct a malefic, particularly Saturn, and found in the fourth, eighth, or twelfth house, the parents are tragic figures whose fate leaves deep emotional scars on the native. Later in life, others he loves dearly may suffer tragic fates. This is a literary degree and is often found accented in the charts of writers whose novels, plays, or occult works have a lasting emotional effect upon their readers.

Scheat, a second magnitude star at 28 Pisces 30, is said to have malevolence of "sublime scope." It is frequently on the MC or otherwise prominent in the charts of people condemned to death, life imprisonment, or bondage.

9. *The Decanates.* Each sign is divided into three parts of ten degrees called decanates. Each decanate has a ruler that becomes a sub-ruler of the sign. If a planet happens to fall in a decanate it rules, it is considered to have an essential dignity by which its power is increased. Unfortunately, if the whole sign is detrimental to the planet, the fact that it may be placed in a decanate of that sign which it rules may increase its power for evil if it is a malefic and badly aspected.

There are two methods for determining the planetary rulers of the decanates. The simplest and most commonly used by modern astrologers is by triplicity. In this system, the first sign of the Fire triplicity is Aries. Therefore, the first ten degrees is the Aries decanate, ruled by Mars, the second is the Leo decanate, ruled by the Sun, and the third is the Sagittarius decanate, ruled by Jupiter. In the Earth triplicity, the first sign is Taurus, and the first ten degrees are ruled by Venus, the second ten by Mercury, ruler of the next Earth sign, and the third is the Capricorn decanate, ruled by Saturn. And so on.

A convenience of this method is that it gives us an opportunity to give minor essential dignities to the three outer planets. Thus, in the Air triplicity, Gemini is the first sign. Mercury rules the first ten degrees, Venus (ruler of Libra) the next ten, and the last ten, the Aquarian decanate, could be assigned to Uranus. This is informative because the last ten degrees of Gemini have often been called a decanate of genius. If it is legitimate to do this, the first decanate of Cancer would be ruled by the Moon, the second by Pluto, and the third by Neptune. This may help to explain the drive to accumulate enormous wealth that is commonly found in the second decanate, and the sometimes pronounced psychic and artistic abilities, as well as the tendency to martyrdom, often found in the last.

The other system, called the Chaldean rulerships, is incredibly ancient. The decanates are assigned rulerships in the order of the planets from Saturn inward to the Moon, as in the table on the next page.

Read across, these are the Chaldean rulers of the decanates. Read down, they are the rulers of the days of the week and also the order of the rulers of the planetary hours. These may be important in horary astrology, especially in event charts. A "planetary hour" lasts two hours of clock time, and the counting starts not from midnight, but from sunrise. For convenience we consider this to be 6:00 a.m., which is rather arbitrary because sunrise varies a good deal with the time of year and the latitude. The first planetary hour, from 6 a.m. to 8 a.m., is assigned to the ruler of the day. The order then follows automatically. Thus, the first planetary hour of any Wednesday is ruled by Mercury, the second by Jupiter, the third by Venus, and so on through twelve planetary hours or twenty-four hours of clock time. You will notice this automatically makes Jupiter the ruler of

	The Chaldean Decanates					
Sign			*Faces (Decanates)*			
Aries	0-9	Mars	10-19	Sun	20-29	Venus
Taurus	0-9	Mercury	10-19	Moon	20-29	Saturn
Gemini	0-9	Jupiter	10-19	Mars	20-29	Sun
Cancer	0-9	Venus	10-19	Mercury	20-29	Moon
Leo	0-9	Saturn	10-19	Jupiter	20-29	Mars
Virgo	0-9	Sun	10-19	Venus	20-29	Mercury
Libra	0-9	Moon	10-19	Saturn	20-29	Jupiter
Scorpio	0-9	Mars	10-19	Sun	20-29	Venus
Sagittarius	0-9	Mercury	10-19	Moon	20-29	Saturn
Capricorn	0-9	Jupiter	10-19	Mars	20-29	Sun
Aquarius	0-9	Venus	10-19	Mercury	20-29	Moon
Pisces	0-9	Saturn	10-19	Jupiter	20-29	Mars

the first planetary hour on Thursday, Venus on Friday, Saturn on Saturday, the Sun on Sunday, the Moon on Monday, and Mars on Tuesday.

In my experience, the Chaldean decanates yield excellent descriptive results in natal astrology. They should be part of every student's arsenal of knowledge.

10. Peregrine Planets. Peregrine is an archaic word meaning "to wander footloose, without purpose, to be at loose ends." When a planet is out of all dignity, does not dispose of any other planet, makes no aspects and receives none, it is said to be *peregrine.* It is off by itself, out of communication with the other factors in the chart. It's a dropout from the planetary society and is powerless to influence the outcome of the question. If the ruler of the first house (the querent) is peregrine, he is unable to do anything about the situation he is in. If the ruler of the seventh is peregrine, the astrologer will be unable to find the correct answer. If one of the significators of a person or thing asked about is peregrine, he or it can contribute nothing constructive to the outcome. If the significator of a lost object is peregrine, it will probably never be found, or if found accidentally, it will be damaged beyond repair. Sometimes, the peregrine significator means that the question is not serious, but merely asked from idle curiosity. Sometimes, it means that the matter asked about has already been settled, so the question is pointless. It always means lack of cooperation from whatever or whoever the peregrine planet rules.

Part Two

Introduction

This section deals with important problems and shows how they were solved by horary astrology. Some of these problems, such as questions about real estate, investments, and employment are important because almost everyone has to cope with them at times. Others, such as the threat of imprisonment or the search for a missing person, occur but rarely; however, when they do occur, the situation is of great importance to the client and any insight that may help to avert tragedy or throw light upon a mystery is worthwhile.

The charts used in this section were cast to answer actual questions or to judge actual events. In all cases, the outcome is known, and I have described how the matter worked out so that the student can follow the method and determine how closely the astrological analysis coincided with the development of events and where, in some cases, it fell short of perfection.

There has been no attempt to find examples to fit every house of the horoscope. While it is vitally important that the student learn to place each question in its proper house, this can only be done in relation to each particular question—no two questions are exactly alike. Horary astrology is a method for discovering facts unknown to the querent which will, if the chart is valid, become known in the future. Once the student understands the method, he will have no trouble selecting the proper house for each question.

As an exercise which might be both amusing and profitable, the student can take each of the following charts and imagine that one or more very different questions were asked. Each of these questions would fall in different houses from the one actually asked in the example, and might, therefore, provide a different answer. Since the student knows what actually did happen, he should be able to judge how this outcome might affect his hypothetical question—if it would affect it at all. Of course, this is a game. But it is fun to play, and if undertaken seriously, it facilitates understanding of the horary method and increases one's confidence in its use.

13

Real Estate

Chart 1 is cast for February 2, 1968, at 2:40 p.m., Washington, D.C. The client telephoned me at that time to say he had finally found a house he wanted to buy and planned to put a deposit on it the following morning. Not only did he have to move from the place he was renting, but he also felt that real estate was a good hedge against inflation. His question was: Is it wise to do as I plan and buy this particular house?

In all questions about real estate, the first house rules the buyer, the seventh the seller, the fourth the property, and the tenth the price.

Immediately we see that the Moon ruling the buyer and Saturn ruling the seller are in conjunction in the tenth house, which means that there would be no obstacle to their coming together and agreeing on a price. In fact, with Venus, which always has a connotation of money in questions like this, just below the seventh cusp and only 29 past a square to Saturn, ruling the seller, we could conclude that he was under pressure of necessity to sell and most anxious to do so. Sometimes, the seller's need for money means the buyer gets a bargain, but in all questions where anxiety to sell is plain, the astrologer should look for a reason. Perhaps the seller wants to unload a lemon. Further testimony that there could be ready agreement on price is found in the fact that Mercury, ruler of the property, and Jupiter, ruler of the price, are in mutual reception, with one being in the third house of deeds and papers and the other in the ninth of legal settlements.

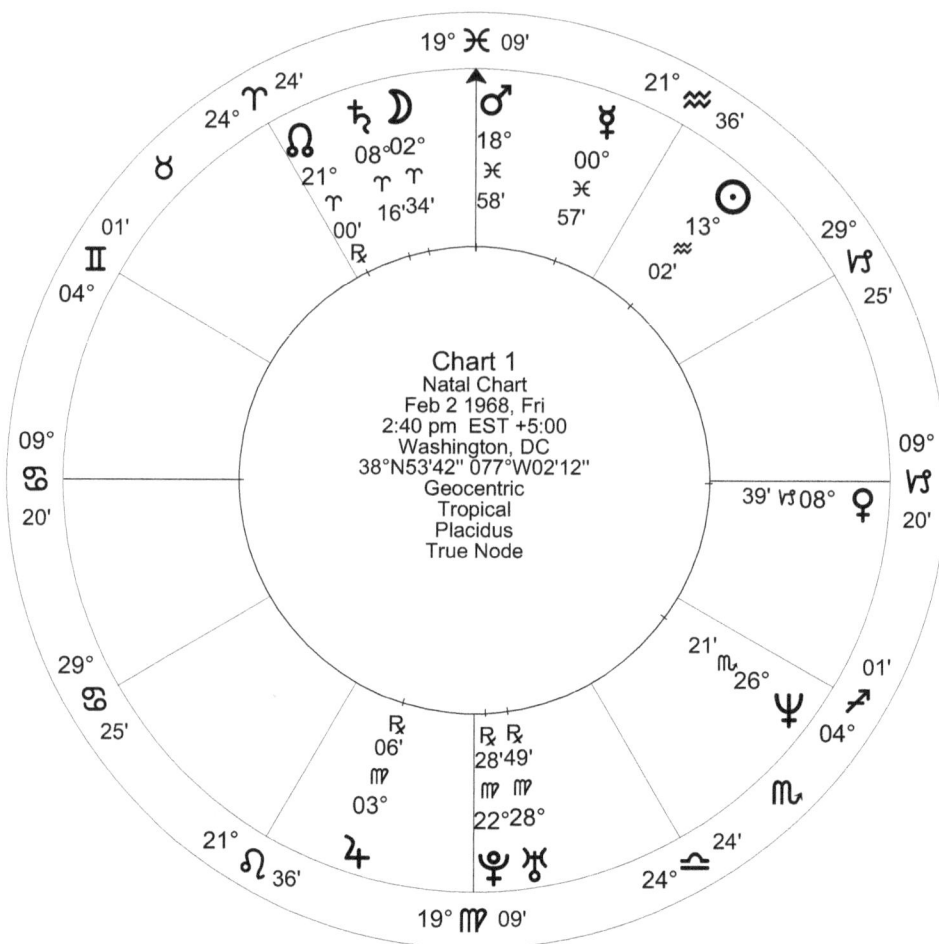

Chart 1. Question: I plan to place a deposit on a house tomorrow. Is this wise?
February 2, 1968, 2:40 p.m. EST, Washington, D.C.

Nevertheless, the client was told not to buy the house, for the following reasons:

1. There was a possibility of death or injury to some member of the family through fire or explosion because Mars (fire) at the tenth cusp was in opposition to Pluto and Uranus in the fourth, with Pluto (death) in the degree of the Nodes (fatality).

2. The value would decline, because Saturn (depreciation, chronic decay) was in the tenth; and the buyer (the Moon) would never be able to get his money out of the house because the Moon was conjunct Saturn (traps, binds). Therefore, this particular house was a poor hedge against inflation.

3. The deal was of more advantage to the seller than to the buyer. He was selling under heavy pressure (Saturn conjunction Moon square Venus) of debt. I was then told the seller was a woman.

4. The title was clouded (Saturn conjunction Moon square Venus) and Mercury (documents, deeds) in Pisces (confusion) opposition Jupiter (legal title). I was told this was probable as the house was very old and built on what had originally been king's grant land. Many such titles were clouded.

5. The heating system was defective (Mars in opposition to Pluto and Uranus). Danger of boiler (Pluto) explosion (Uranus) as cause of number 1. I was told he had noticed this when inspecting the house and planned to put in a new heating system if he bought it.

6. Even if he did this, the possibility of fire from another source, such as *riot* (Pluto) or a flaming object falling from the air onto the roof (Mars at tenth cusp) could not be ruled out. I asked if the house was near an airport (Uranus) because if so it might be vulnerable to a plane crash. I was told it was directly under the route to National Airport and the planes flew very low over it.

7. Something was seriously wrong with the land. The house was built on a swamp or soft fill (Pluto in fourth) and was actually sinking, which was the cause of the problem with the boiler and heating system, and since nothing could be done to remedy the cause, it would be useless to put in a new system. I was told that the house was in Old Town Alexandria, one of a row of pre-revolutionary frame houses that had been built on low, swampy ground that had been inadequately filled. Nevertheless, it was highly prestigious property, and my client had difficulty believing that it would ever decline in value as I predicted.

He followed my advice, however, and did not buy the property. This chart illustrates the value of using the three outer planets to represent things that they do rule, or social conditions in the outside world beyond the immediate scope of the problem, and to use only the seven classical planets as the rulers of the signs. At the time I mentioned *riot* (Pluto) as the possible cause of fire (on February 2, 1968) nothing could have seemed more improbable to a peaceful resident of Old Town Alexandria. Yet, two months later, after the assassination of Martin Luther King Jr., the whole center of Washington was in flames. This assassination was the tragic fatality indicated by Pluto (death) opposition Mars (gunshots) in the degree of the Nodes. There were no riots in Alexandria at that time, however. Sporadic trouble broke out there about a year later and lasted, off and on, for about two years. The house was finally burned to the ground by a firebomb thrown onto the roof from a passing truck full of adolescent blacks. Notice that there is a second mutual reception in this chart: Mars in Pisces and Neptune in Scorpio. Neptune falls in the fifth house of juveniles in the sign Scorpio (delinquents). The arsonists escaped (mutual reception) without punishment because they were juveniles.

On the other mutual reception, my client escaped a bad bargain because he followed the advice of an astrologer.

Another interesting clue in this chart is the condition of the second house. In horary astrology, we look to the fourth house for the final outcome, and to the second for the immediate future.

Here 29 Cancer 27 is on the second-house cusp, indicating that the matter had no future. In this case, it had no future because the querent did not buy the house. But if he had bought, it still would have had no future. It would have been a dead end action resulting in loss and the ultimate necessity to buy another house if he escaped the fire.

Chart 2 also describes a real-estate transaction. This was set up for an event: the moment when the potential buyer first saw the house on March 5, 1959, at 1:00 p.m. in Washington, D.C. Although he had been looking for a house to buy for some time, the first sight of this one was accidental. He happened to walk by it when on the way to inspect another property that had been advertised.

The property was a four-story townhouse, which the seller (seventh house) had repossessed on a defaulted mortgage and was remodeling into four apartments. The buyer approached him immediately and was very well received (Moon, ruler of the first, the buyer, in the seventh, close sextile Mercury, ruling the fourth, the property). When the seller learned that the buyer wanted the property as a private residence, he quoted a moderate price that was well within the buyer's means. He had already put new bathrooms in on each floor, but selling the house as a residence meant that he could avoid the expense of putting in four kitchens as well as the extensive, and costly, fireproofing required by the building code for apartments.

All the initial transactions went smoothly and quickly. Mercury and Venus, the two rulers of the fourth, were moving into a conjunction in the tenth (the price). Mercury was in a close trine Jupiter and was in mutual reception with Mars. Venus was moving from a sextile to Mars, which disposed of her into a trine to Uranus, which was in the buyer's second house of finances. Uranus in this position indicated some fortunate, but unknown, condition in the external world that was beyond the control of either the buyer or the seller and which would work to the financial advantage of both.

A conventional mortgage was arranged with incredible speed on terms highly favorable to the buyer. He was quite ignorant of Washington property values, and, as a newcomer to the city, knew nothing about the desirability of any particular neighborhood. The one where the house was located was actually rather run down and to all appearances property there would decline in value. The unknown Uranian factor contradicted this superficial appearance, however. The bank providing the mortgage knew that land values in the neighborhood were rising at a fantastically rapid rate (Venus in the tenth trine Uranus in the second) because big real-estate firms were buying up whole blocks of decayed houses for demolition with the intention of building high-rise luxury apartments and office buildings. The bank's appraiser, therefore, evaluated the property at 25 percent more than the seller's asking price.

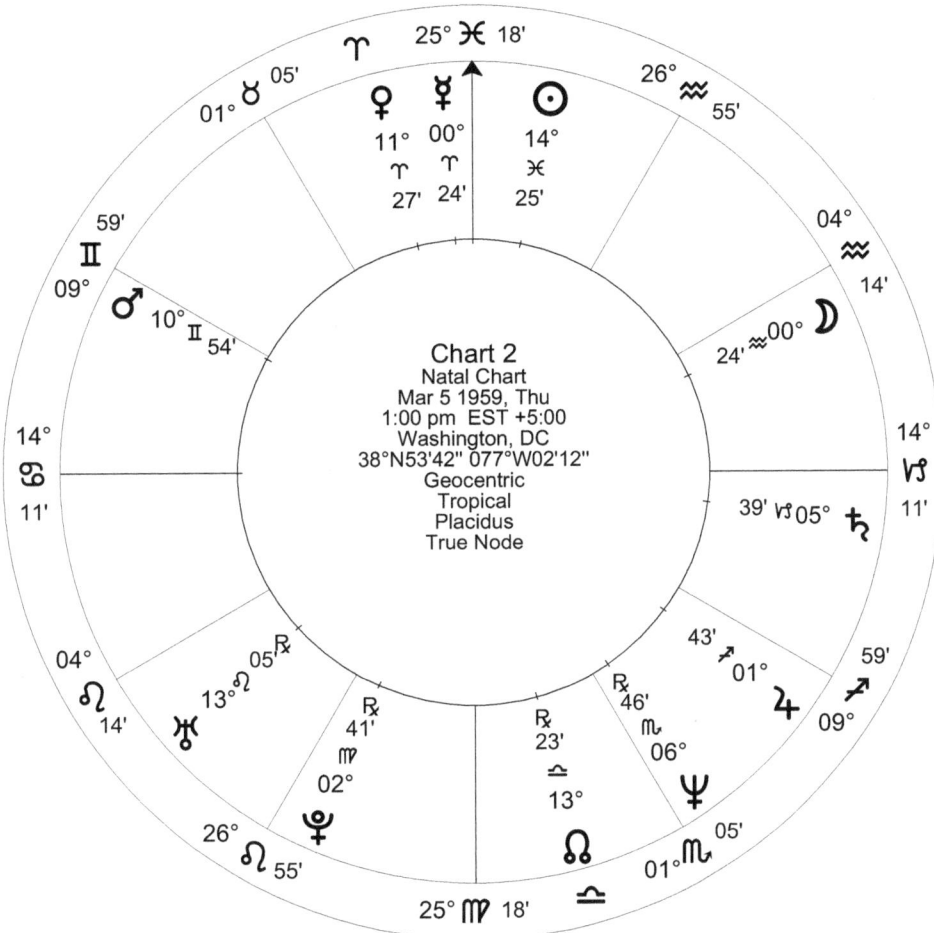

Chart 2. Event: Client first saw a house he might buy.
March 5, 1959, 1 p.m. EST, Washington, D.C.

There was no doubt that this property was an excellent bargain for the buyer. Nevertheless, there were many delays in his taking possession of it. They arose because the seller was a liar (Mercury square Saturn, his ruler, and sextile the Moon). The seller was psychologically unable to tell the truth about anything, or to avoid the temptation to indulge in shady dealings. Because it was his nature to be dishonest and to lie, he had got himself into desperate financial straits, so the sooner he got the cash for this house, the better off he would be, and the better able to rescue himself from some of his other misfortunes. He seemed unable to realize this, however, and he actually took deposits on this house, after it had been sold to the first buyer, from *three* other people! None of them was able to arrange a mortgage, fortunately, or the wheeler-dealer seller might have gone to jail. But, while collecting deposit money from everyone willing to give him some, he dawdled over finishing the work he had agreed to do to make the house habitable. Naturally, the actual buyer refused to complete the transaction and take title to the property until this work was done. Instead of taking title in May, as had been promised, the matter was delayed until August, when the transit Sun formed the conjunction to Uranus, coruler of the ninth (legal title).

Meanwhile, as the work haltingly progressed, the seller refused to pay the bills for material and labor. Mercury square Saturn can indicate a thief as well as a liar. If the buyer had not had astrological advice throughout this whole period, he might have been held liable for several thousand dollars of mechanics liens. But, having been warned by the astrologer that the seller would undoubtedly leave all the construction bills unpaid, the buyer took out title insurance. He had good reason to be thankful for this because, during the first year he lived in the house, he discovered that he might have been liable for a two thousand dollar plumbing bill and even more for lumber and other materials.

Notice in this chart that the Sun and the Ascendant are both in the degree of the Moon's Nodes, an indication of fatality. The buyer lived the rest of his life happily in this house. He was then killed in an accident while at work. His wife inherited the property, which has about tripled in value since 1959 (Venus in the tenth trine Uranus, and Mercury in the tenth trine Jupiter).

14

Employment

Chart 3 is for an event: the offer of a job on May 14, 1970, at 3:10 p.m. EDT, Washington, D.C. The question was: Should the client accept the job?

About six months before this event, the client had come on a routine visit to have his progressions and transits checked for 1970. For several years, he had been having trouble with his marriage and kept claiming that he wanted a divorce. But when I gave him dates on which he could start proceedings with the expectation of the greatest success with the least friction, he always managed to evade the issue. This time when he came, he announced that nothing had changed since his last visit in any of the matters that bothered him: he had not got a divorce, his finances were still in a mess, he was still involved in a law suit over a real estate deal, he still hadn't been able to buy an apartment building he wanted—in short, everything was exactly the same as on his last visit except that he had bought the property in Jamaica which I had advised him not to buy. So what should he do now?

I told him that nothing had changed in his life because he had not done a single thing about any of his problems. It was clear that he did not really want a divorce because he would have to straighten out his financial affairs to make the necessary settlement on his wife. If he got a divorce, he would be free to marry his mistress, which he did not want to do. In any case, I told him, his marriage was no longer his major problem. The focus had shifted to his job. I told him that within three weeks to a month he would be fired without notice, that he would be out of

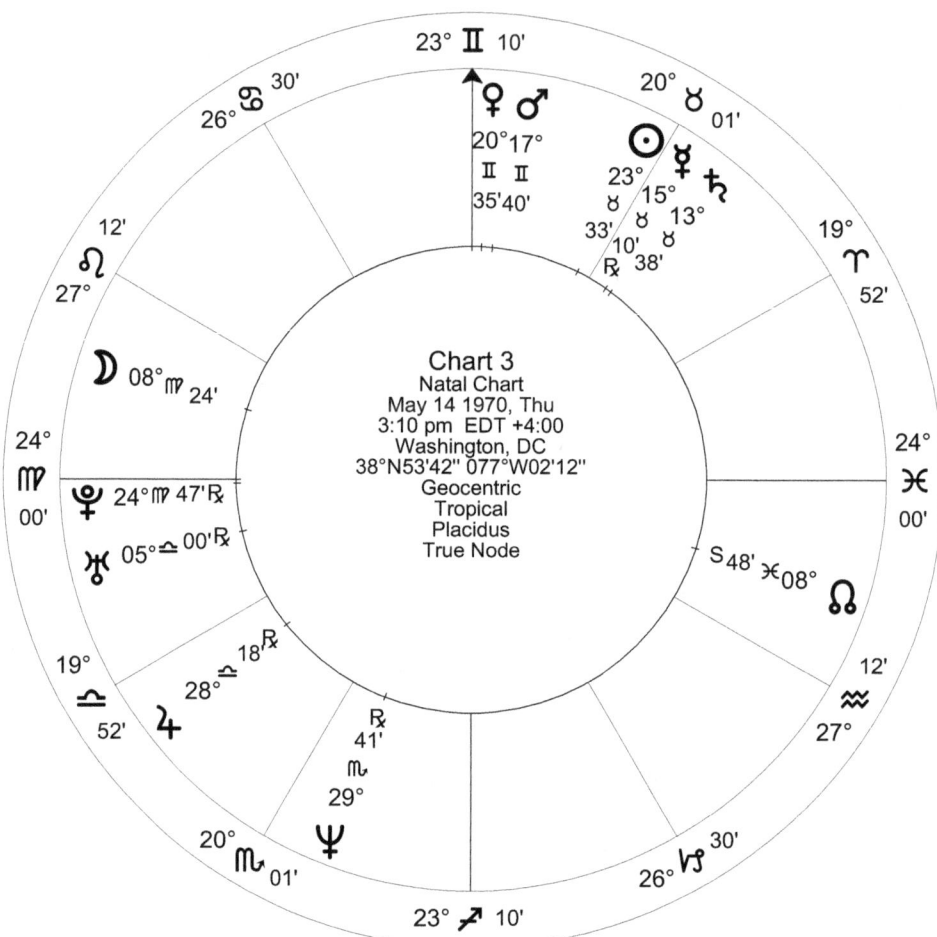

Chart 3. Event: Offer of a job, May 14, 1970, 3:10 p.m. EDT, Washington, D.C.

work for some time, possibly a year, and that he had better get his financial affairs in order, sell the Jamaica property and some of his antiques, put the money in insured savings accounts where he could get it in a hurry, and start looking for another job. This analysis was made on the basis of his natal chart, and the solar arcs and transits over it.

He found my prediction ridiculous. He had worked for the same large corporation for more than twenty years, was in charge of their Washington office for a salary of over $50,000 a year; his principal duty was to lobby for government contracts, and he was so successful at this that there was no prospect he would ever be fired. I insisted that in spite of his firm's affection for him, they would close down their Washington office and have no further use for him. He left, extremely dissatisfied with the interview, and I'm sure with astrology in general.

Three weeks later, I had a call from his mistress. She told me he was too distraught to talk to me. That morning the company's vice president had flown into Washington to tell him they were closing down the office because the Vietnam War was winding down and the Defense Department was cancelling contracts. He had a week to move out, a few months of severance pay, and they would do all they could to help him find another job. His faith in astrology was restored. He'd do anything "the stars" said, if only I'd help him get another job. I repeated what I'd told him about getting his finances in order and added that whenever he got an offer, he should note down the exact date and time. I would then set up a horary chart for the event and we could judge whether it would be to his advantage to accept.

Chart 3 is for the first offer he had. It came to him without effort on his part from the president of the company, who had heard that he was out of work and felt that his long experience in obtaining government contracts was just what the company needed. My client was most enthusiastic about the offer, which was to pay him $75,000 a year to reorganize the sales department plus a generous commission on all contracts from our own or foreign governments. That was all he told me about the matter. I did not even know what the company manufactured.

I told him to refuse the offer.

Since this is the chart for an event, the first house rules the person taking the initial action—in this case, the president of the company who had voluntarily made the offer. Here, the first house is ruled by retrograde Mercury in the eighth house of death and loss and conjunct Saturn. A retrograde Pluto (death) is rising. I told him the president was a very old man, ill, close to death. The Moon (function) is in the old man's twelfth but also in Virgo, so it was acting on the hidden side of the first. The old man was stubbornly running a very antiquated business (Mercury conjunct Saturn) and refused to tell anyone how it functioned. The business was an old-fashioned, one-man show. The president was too old and too ill to manage it, but too jealous of his power to delegate authority to anyone else.

My client said, "That's all true. That's why he wants me to come in to run it."

I pointed out that the old man's dictatorial ways and paranoid secrecy had got things in an irretrievable mess (Moon in twelfth conjunct the South Node and the Part of Fortune also in the degree of the Nodes.) It wasn't only the old man who was going to die—the whole business was dying along with him. If my client accepted, he would have to move to another city, which would put him to great expense. He would no sooner get there than the whole thing would collapse (Mercury retrograde). My client said that was true: he would have to move to Chicago.

This potential and undesirable move is shown by the condition of the Sun. The seventh house here rules my client, to whom the offer was made. Therefore, the sixth from the seventh, which is the twelfth, rules his employment in this job. The Sun (twelfth ruler) falls in the third from the seventh, indicating a new environment that would not live up to what was promised for it because the Sun, although trine Pluto, was opposing Neptune (delusion or deceit). The trine of the Sun to Pluto (the old dictator) had got him the offer, but the old man could never make good on his promise because Pluto was retrograde. After he moved, he would simply have to return to his present home (the fourth from the seventh) because Mercury, its ruler, was retrograde.

Actually, I told him, the firm was near bankruptcy. (Retrograde Jupiter in the second and the Sun opposing Neptune.)

The last planet the Moon conjoined was Venus in Gemini, which was also just past a conjunction with Mars, ruler of the eighth of bankruptcy. From this, I judged that there had been talk of a merger with or sale to a larger corporation as a last ditch effort to save some of the stockholders' money. I said the old man had children and grandchildren who were in favor of this. With Capricorn on the old man's fifth-house cusp, Saturn rules his children. It is in the eighth house of bankruptcy conjunct Mercury, which is in mutual reception with Venus (arbitration) and receiving a trine from the Moon. My client said it was true that a large corporation had offered to buy the business and the old man had had a big fight with his sons over it. They insisted, correctly, that it was the only way to save anything. But the old man said they were good-for-nothing wastrels who would do anything to get out of working, and he'd be damned if he'd sell out just so they could take their share and waste it on gambling and riotous living!

I then asked if the company manufactured products of lead or stone, or some other very heavy material. (Mercury ruling the company—tenth house—conjunct Saturn in Taurus.) This is about the heaviest combination one could imagine, so whatever the company did, I thought it must have something to do with weight.

My client laughed and said the company made scales! Mercury rules measuring instruments, Saturn rules weight, and Taurus rules the force of gravity! They were, in fact, one of the oldest manufacturers of scales in the country and still turned out finely calibrated precision-weighing machines that, due to the large amount of hand labor involved in making them, had become too high priced for the market.

My client refused the job. The next time I saw him he told me that the old man had died, leaving everything in an incredible mess, and that his heirs had reopened negotiations with the large corporation to buy the business, but on terms much less favorable than they could have negotiated when the deal was first proposed.

Chart 4 was drawn for the moment the client opened a letter offering him a job as a research scientist working for the U.S. Navy. The time was 10:05 a.m. EST, October 12, 1960, Washington, D.C. In this case, the first house rules the man who received the offer because he had initiated the action that led to it. The offer came as the result of a long, discouraging search for employment, during which he had applied to many private corporations and government agencies. He had rejected three previous offers received at times that yielded hopelessly bad charts. At the

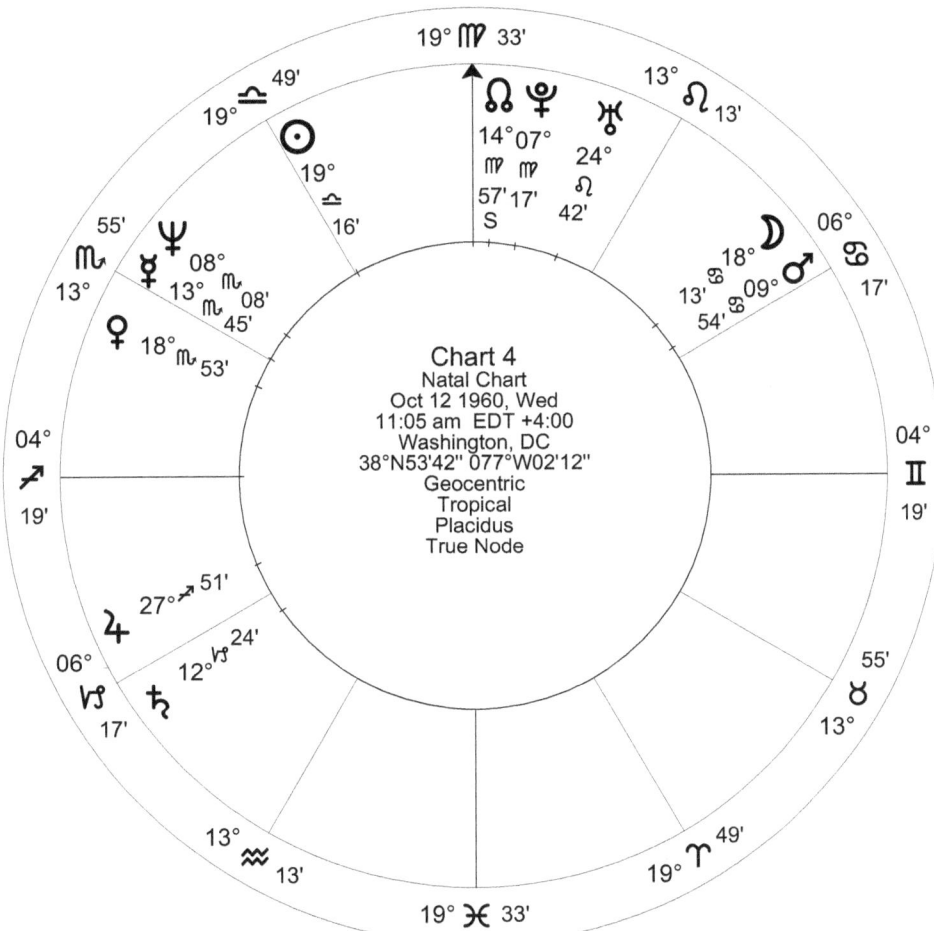

Chart 4. Event: Job offered in response to client's actively seeking it.
October 12, 1960, 10:05 a.m. EST, Washington, D.C.

time this offer arrived, he was ill with a serious infection and beginning to feel financially pinched from four months of unemployment. Therefore, in spite of the difficulties shown in this chart, he decided to pursue the matter and take this job if he could get it.

It turned out that the Navy was anxious to hire him in spite of the poor condition of his health at the moment, because the research pertained to a new, highly secret project for which top secret clearance was necessary. In this respect, he had a clean record. This circumstance shows clearly in the chart in the condition of the sixth house (his employment). The ruler, Venus, is in Scorpio (secret investigation or research) in the twelfth (secrets). The Moon (function) is in the mute sign Cancer in the secret eighth house, and the first aspect it makes is a trine to Venus. Mercury, ruler of those making the offer (seventh house) is also in Scorpio at the twelfth-house cusp.

Notice that there are no retrograde planets here. This rare but highly desirable condition no doubt did much to help overcome the serious difficulties shown by Mars opposing Saturn and the Moon square the Sun. Actually, he was so critically ill when the offer was received that he could not begin work until four months later, and for several months thereafter, he was still not strong enough to stand up all day in the laboratory to do the work for which he had been hired. Yet, his new employers remained unfailingly considerate and patient, doing everything possible to help him through this difficult period.

Nevertheless, as time passed, friction did develop with his immediate supervisors because of these two quarrelsome aspects. In about eight years, when Mars by solar arc reached the conjunction to the Moon, this continued friction made him unhappy, because he felt it interfered with his work, so he was once more looking for another job. Before he found one, however, Mars by solar arc reached the square to the Sun, and he was killed in a laboratory explosion. Because of the highly secret nature of the work, nothing the investigation into the causes of this disaster turned up has ever been revealed. The astrologer is, therefore, at liberty to draw his own conclusions from the testimony of the chart.

Notice that Mercury on the twelfth-house cusp is in the degree of the Nodes—fatality.

15

Travel

Chart 5 is set up for the moment when a United Air Lines passenger jet took off from National Airport at 1:40 p.m. EST on December 8, 1972. Chart 6 is set up for the moment it crashed into a block of houses on the edge of Midway Airport, Chicago, Illinois, at 2:29 p.m. CST. Forty-six people, out of sixty-one on the plane, were killed.

In a travel chart, the first house rules the ship, aircraft, bus, spacecraft, or train that is the means of travel and carries the passengers. The Moon rules the passengers. The Sun rules the captain, engineer, pilot, or driver of the vessel or vehicle who is responsible for its safe conduct. The fourth house rules the point of departure, the seventh rules the area traversed, the ports of call, and the adventures encountered on the way. The tenth rules the destination, or, in old-fashioned language, the fate of the journey and passengers. With our modern orientation toward belief in free will, we are inclined to forget the classical meaning of the tenth; it is the house of Fate. But wherever people entrust their lives and fortunes to someone else whose actions and judgment are beyond their control, as is the case when we embark upon a plane or ship, this ancient meaning of the tenth house comes into play. If there is a crew, they are ruled by the sixth house.

The ruler of the takeoff chart is Mars in Scorpio. The only aspect in longitude Mars can make before it leaves the sign is a quincunx (fatality) to Saturn, ruler of the tenth (destination). All the planets that move faster than Mars have gone beyond it, and Mars itself has gone beyond the

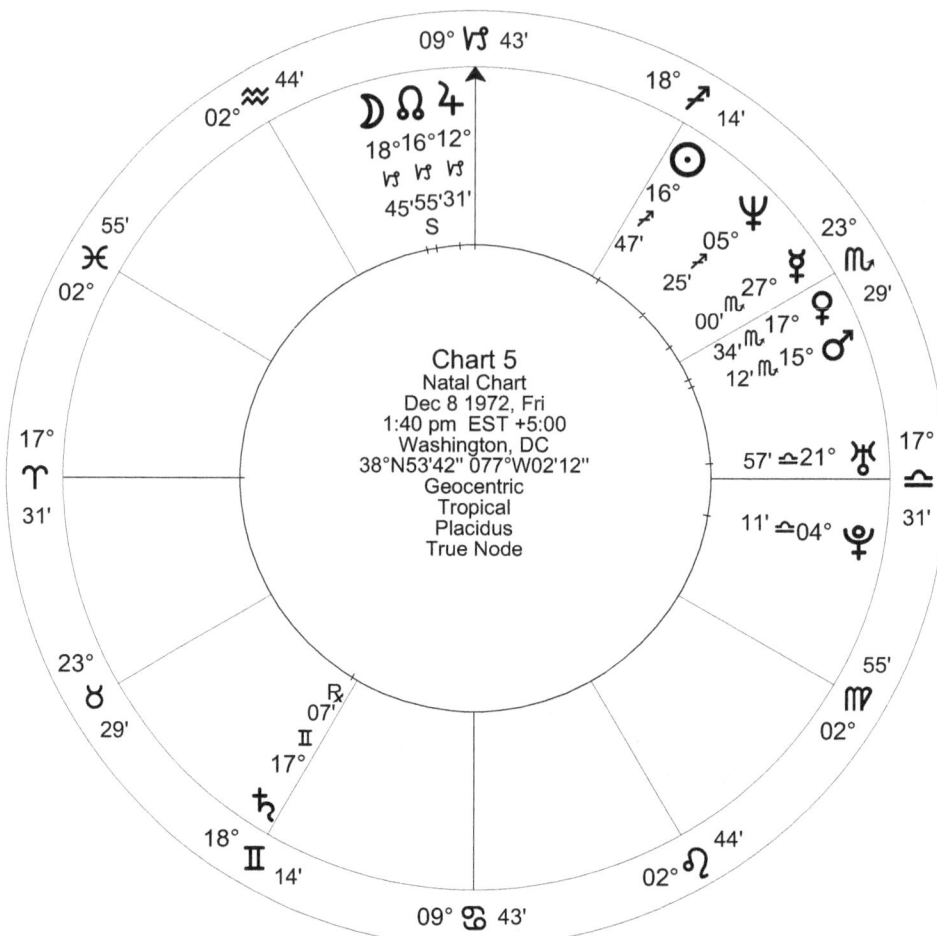

Chart 5. Event: Takeoff of plane. December 8, 1972, 1:40 p.m. EST, Washington, D.C.

sextile to Jupiter. However, in declination, Mars is parallel Venus and contraparallel Pluto, which disposes of both of them and rules the eighth house of death.

The Moon (passengers) is in Capricorn in the tenth (destination) in the degree of the Nodes (fatality). It is also in the degree of the eclipse of the Sun, which occurred on July 10, 1972. It is moving from a quincunx to Saturn (fatality) to a square with Uranus, ruler of aircraft, in general, and of sudden disasters. The Ascendant (this particular aircraft) is applying to a square to the Moon, an opposition to Uranus, and is but 12 minutes from an exact quincunx (fatality) to Venus, ruler of the seventh (the journey). The double quincunx formed to two points that are sextile each other is called the Yod, or "finger of God" aspect and is associated with Fate. People who believe that their destinies are entirely under their own personal control generally avoid

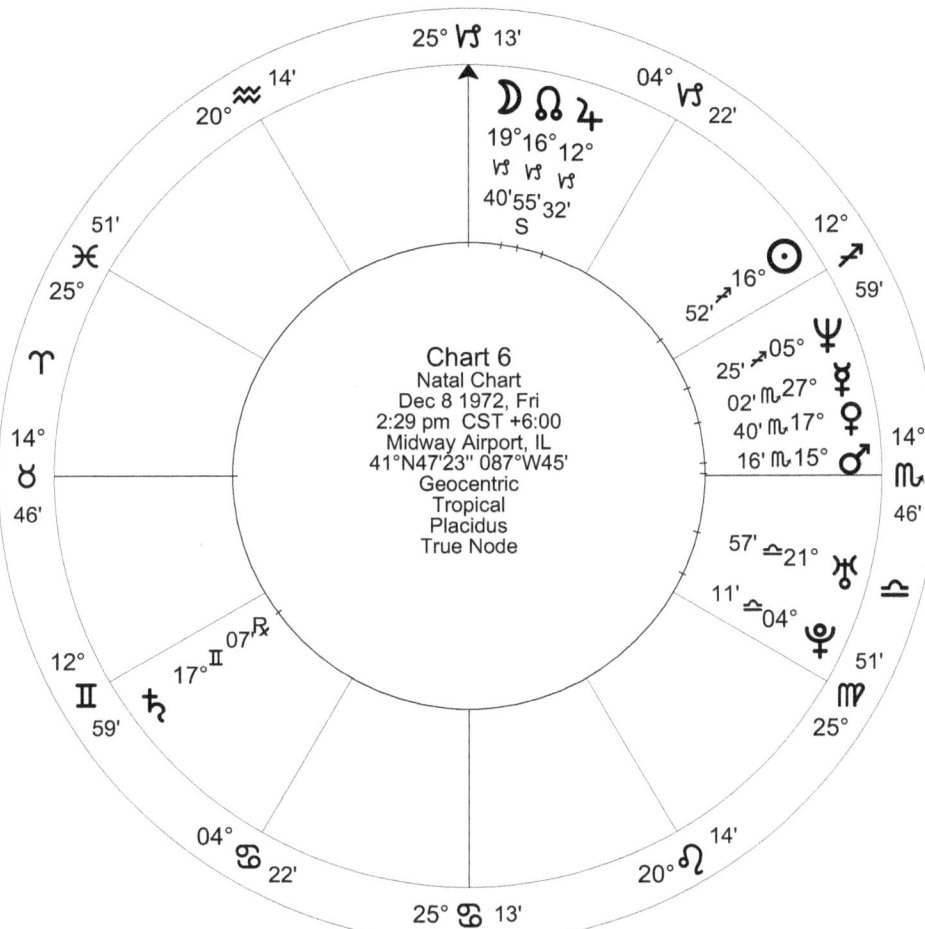

Chart 6. Event: Plane crash. December 8, 1972, 2:29 p.m. CST, Chicago IL.

any discussion of it, for it makes them uncomfortable. The Moon, past sextile Venus, forms another Yod with Venus and Saturn. Since the Moon is also past the quincunx to Saturn, an optimist might conclude that whatever trouble it indicated was over—a past fatality. An interesting sidelight on this interpretation is that a family of five killed in the crash was returning home after having attended a funeral! But although the quincunx of the Moon to Saturn is past in longitude, it is still operating because the Moon and Saturn are contraparallel. I find that parallels and contraparallels usually act in the manner of the closest aspect they form in longitude.

This combination of influences affecting the passengers, their destination, and the journey itself are rather strong testimony that a mishap on the journey would prevent them from reaching their destination.

The Sun (the pilot or captain) is opposition to Saturn (falls). Except for the quincunx of Venus to the Ascendant, this is the closest applying aspect in the chart and testifies that the pilot wouldn't reach his destination either. Saturn, ruler of the end of the journey, is the only retrograde planet in the chart. Retrograde planets never end up where they seem to be going.

Mercury, ruling the crew, is at the end of Scorpio, making no aspects to anything before it leaves the sign. This means the crew was powerless to do anything to help avert the disaster.

There are two interesting midpoints. The Moon was moving into a quincunx to the midpoint of Saturn and Uranus, which is 19 Leo 32. At the time of the crash, this aspect was 8 degrees past partile. Jupiter is square the midpoint between Uranus and Pluto, which is 13 Libra 07.

There was additional warning in the antiscion degrees, which are sometimes called solstice points. The antiscion of a planet is its distance from either end of the solstice axis, 0 Capricorn-Cancer, on the other side of the axis. The antiscion of Saturn is 12 Cancer 52, opposition Jupiter, indicating a fall from great heights. The antiscion of the Sun is 13 Capricorn 12 square the Uranus-Pluto midpoint. The antiscion of the Moon is 11 Sagittarius 16 conjunct the Sun-Neptune midpoint, which is 11 Sagittarius 06. The antiscion of Venus is 12 Leo 25, quincunx Jupiter.

At the time of the crash, the Ascendant had moved to 14 Taurus 46 from an opposition to Mars on the Descendant. The MC had become 25 Capricorn 13, which was just past a conjunction with the antiscion of Neptune at 24 Capricorn 35. There was a misty rain and the visibility was poor, both afflictions of Neptune.

In judging whether one should take a particular flight, look to the condition of the Ascendant, the Moon, and the ruler of the tenth. Try to avoid quincunxes, especially double ones—the Yod. Never start a journey when the Moon is in the degree of its Nodes. And pick a time when the rulers of the Ascendant and the tenth are not retrograde.

This chart holds another lesson for the student of horary astrology: Jupiter at the MC is not enough to solve all problems and make everything come out right in the end. It cannot overcome the dead-end results of a void-of-course Moon or the fatality promised by multiple quincunxes plus planets in the degree of the Nodes. In such cases, optimism based solely on a tenth-house Jupiter is unwarranted. The best it can do is to ensure that you will get your name in the papers.

Chart 7 is a tragic one, drawn for the moment the Titanic sailed on its maiden voyage from Southampton, at 12:15 p.m. GMT, April 10, 1912. The data are from Lloyd's Shipping Column in the *London Times* for April 11.

The map contains most of the classical warnings of disaster: a void-of-course Moon; a malefic (Neptune) in the degree of the Nodes and square them; the Sun conjunction the North Node;

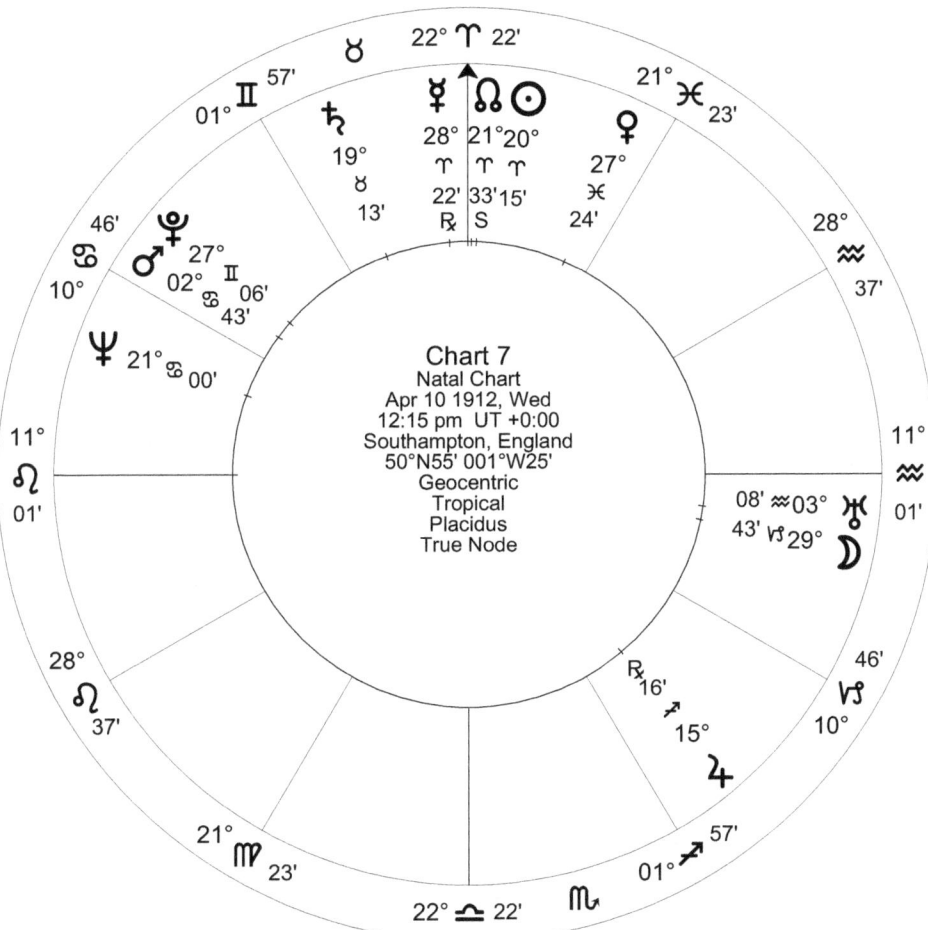

Chart 7. Event: Titanic sailed from Southampton. April 10, 1912, at 12:15 p.m. GMT.

Mars, ruler of the tenth (destination) quincunx Uranus, ruler of the seventh (the voyage); a retrograde Mercury in the tenth; Saturn, symbol of falls and sinking, intercepted in the tenth; the great stars Spica and Arcturus at the Nadir, close to the South Node and opposing the Sun. Jupiter and Sagittarius are always general significators of long voyages. Here, Jupiter is retrograde, and although it is forming a trine to the Ascendant, it makes no planetary aspect to anything in the chart, and it cannot make one, except to the Moon, during the scheduled course of the voyage.

This trine of Jupiter to the Ascendant (the vessel) describes the overblown reputation of the ship and the confidence everyone had in it. It was the largest luxury liner that had been built up to that time. It embodied new concepts of design which were purported to make it unsinkable. It was to

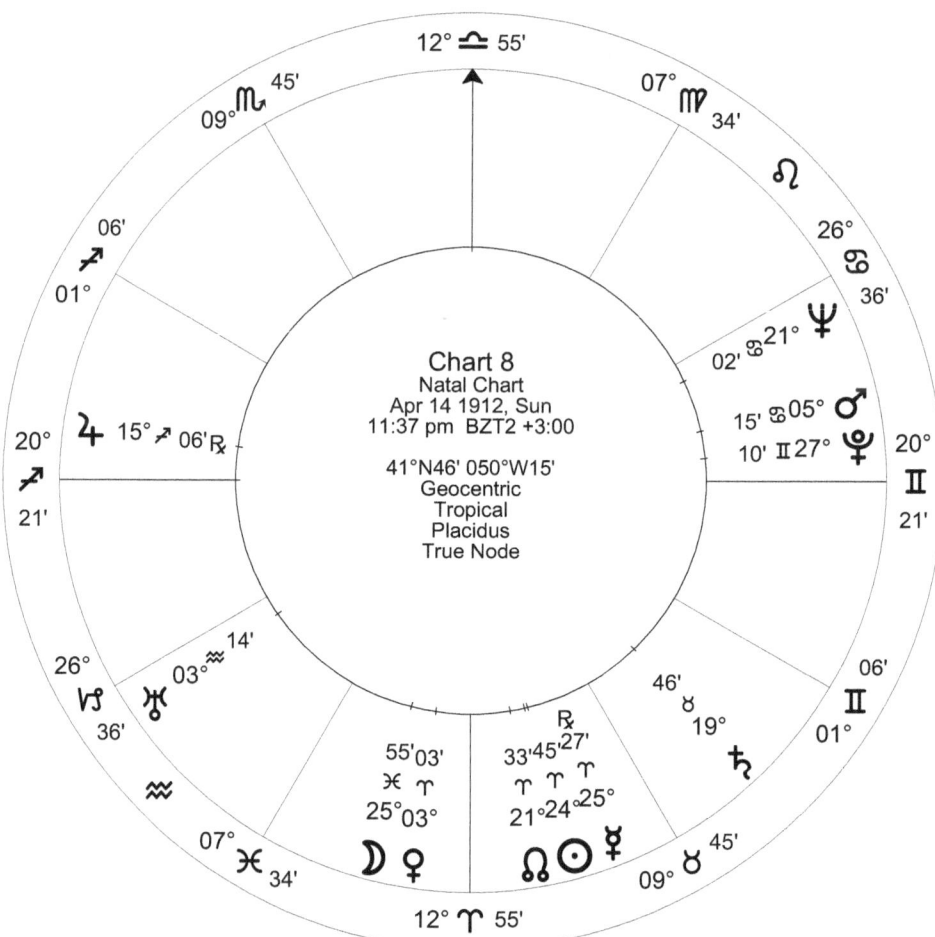

Chart 8. Event: Titanic hit iceberg. April 14, 1912, 11:37 p.m.

set a new record for speed in the North Atlantic passage. It was advertised as the biggest, fastest, safest, most luxurious ship afloat: boasting typical of fire signs and Jupiter trines. But these were all promises never fulfilled, because Jupiter was retrograde and so was Mercury in Aries.

Chart 8 is unusual because it contains only one favorable applying aspect: the sextile between Mercury and Pluto. Sextiles in travel charts are of questionable value and may actually be danger signals if the map is otherwise unfortunate. The reason is that four times each day, as the Earth turns, the angles will form double quincunxes, the dangerous Yod aspect, to the sextiling planets. The Moon will also form a Yod to them if the voyage lasts long enough. Assuming the event chart warns of danger, the disaster will probably occur at one of these times. This was the case with the Titanic. When it sank, the MC was in the 26th degree of Scorpio.

Another interesting feature of the chart is the number of close bad aspects that are just past: Venus square Pluto, the Moon square Mercury, the Part of Fortune conjunct Saturn, the MC 23 conjunct the North Node and square Neptune. All this probably meant that conditions prevailing in the very recent past doomed the ship. Among them were, perhaps, the position of the iceberg (Neptune), structural defects in the vessel that would cause malfunctioning (Moon square Mercury), and preconditioned overoptimism in the Captain (the Sun).

The closest applying aspects in the chart were Mars quincunx Uranus (collision), 26′ from partile; and the Sun, ruling both ship and captain, 45′ from partile square to Neptune (icebergs) in the twelfth house of submergence. In addition to these, Jupiter was afflicted by a contraparallel with Neptune, and the Moon (the passengers) was afflicted by a contraparallel with Mars.

The most dangerous midpoints were those between the Moon and Sun at 10 Pisces, quincunx the Ascendant; the Sun and the North Node at 21 Aries exact square Neptune, and Mars-Pluto at 29 Gemini 25, quincunx the Moon. There were also some very serious antiscion positions. Saturn antiscion was 10 Leo 47, conjunction the Ascendant; Mercury antiscion was 1 Virgo 28, quincunx the Moon-Uranus midpoint; Pluto antiscion was 2 Cancer 55, conjunction Mars; Neptune antiscion was 8 Gemini 55, conjunction the Saturn-Pluto midpoint; South Node antiscion was 10 Pisces 13 quincunx the Ascendant; Uranus antiscion was 26 Scorpio 51, quincunx Pluto and conjunction the MC when the ship sank; and Venus antiscion was 2 Libra 34, square Mars.

Carelli's (*360 Degrees of the Zodiac* by Adriano Carelli) symbolism for two of the degrees involved is interesting. Of 23 Aries (the MC), he says, "A degree of fatality of collective Karma." And of 16 Sagittarius (Jupiter): "A narrow, dark, and deserted blind alley littered with broken toys. An evil influence."

This symbolism of Jupiter's degree, his position in the fifth house of fun and games, and his happy trine to the Ascendant are descriptive of the first class passengers' (Jupiter) attitude toward the ship and the voyage. To get passage on this prestige ship was a status symbol. There was a scalper's market in tickets, and many people paid premium prices for them. Once on board, there was great interest in the ship's speed and heavy betting on whether it would break the previous North Atlantic record, and if so, by how much. The excessive speed of the ship was one of the factors involved in the collision. The Captain (Sun in Aries) was overly anxious to set a new record and unwisely increased the speed to 22 knots after the ship had entered the ice fields. He had iceberg warnings and their positions from other ships in the area, but, with the overconfidence of Aries, he did not take them seriously enough.

A curious blindness or delusion (Sun square Neptune) runs through this whole event. The high powered binoculars that should have been part of the ship's equipment were not put aboard, so the lookouts actually could not see the iceberg at night. There were not enough life boats or life preservers, presumably because everyone believed the ship was actually unsinkable. A wireless from another ship giving the iceberg's position was mislaid and lay on the operator's table for two days before it was given to the captain; by then they were on top of the iceberg. And worst of all was the blind, misplaced confidence in the Titanic's great safety feature, supposed to be a miracle of engineering design.

This was a series of watertight bulkheads built across the width of the ship. Each chamber was walled off from the next to make it water tight, so that if the ship hit anything, water would get into only one chamber and the others would keep it afloat. Unfortunately, these chambers, watertight at the sides, were not watertight at the top. The iceberg raked the ship's bottom, filling a number of these chambers with water and the weight of it tipped the ship down at one end. The water then overflowed from the top of one chamber into the next before engulfing the boiler room, the steerage, and finally the whole ship.

Titanic sank at 2:20 a.m. on April 15 at the same longitude and latitude where it struck the iceberg. At that time, the Ascendant was 1 Aquarius 53, conjunct Uranus. The MC was 25 Scorpio quincunx Mercury and Pluto, and the Moon had reached an exact square to Pluto.

The Titanic was launched on May 31, 1911. The planetary positions at noon that day were: Sun 8 Gemini 54, conjunct the Saturn-Pluto midpoint at the sailing. Moon 24 Cancer 30, square the Sun at the collision. Mercury was at 14 Taurus 43, Venus at 20 Cancer 50 conjunct Neptune and square the Sun at the sailing. Mars was at 28 Pisces 15, with the Venus-Pluto square, at the sailing, applying to it. Jupiter was retrograde at 6 Scorpio 12. Saturn was 13 Taurus 33, with the Ascendant at sailing squaring it. Retrograde Uranus was at 29 Capricorn 04 conjunct the Moon at sailing. Neptune was 19 Cancer 45 sextile Saturn at sailing. Pluto was 26 Gemini square the Moon at collision, and quincunx the MC at sinking. The North Node was 8 Taurus 28 in the degree of the Sun at launching and of the Pluto-Saturn midpoint at sailing. This means the South Node in Scorpio was quincunx both these points. At sailing, the Mercury-Saturn midpoint was 8 Taurus 47, right on the Nodes for launching.

I am sometimes told that this type of practical astrology is "negative." Many students of esoteric and mystical astrology maintain that all is for the best in this best of all possible worlds; that we should never take the responsibility of warning a client of danger, for this might influence his actions and interfere with some Karmic experience that is necessary for his development. According to this view, we should let our clients go ahead and crash their cars, break their legs, fall into bankruptcy, or die of cancer even though *we* see the danger signals clear and loud. These are merely mundane earthly experiences, the inconvenient trash of the material world. We should never try to help a client evade them because, if his Karma has scheduled them for him, it means they are good for his soul.

The first objection to this viewpoint is that it is fatalistic. To let anyone move blindly into disaster, which you can see, is to deprive him of the freedom to make a choice that he might make if he knew the danger was there. Possibly, we do not have freewill, but I do not know this. Whether we have or not is not something I can prove. I do think, however, that people who believe they have some freedom of will and some power to think about and choose their course lead happier and more fruitful lives than those who believe that everything is preordained and that they are slaves of fate.

The second objection to this viewpoint is its arrogance. Who am I to judge the state of another's soul, or to say that misery is good for it? For all I know, his Karma might best be served by struggling against his difficulty and overcoming it. How can he do this if I refuse to admit the problem is there and so deny him the chance to conquer it?

The third objection to this viewpoint is its irresponsibility. When the astrologer takes a client, he accepts both a fee and many very personal revelations and confidences. In return for his money and his trust, the client has every right to expect the astrologer to be honest with him. By accepting the fee and the trust, the astrologer makes himself responsible, in some degree, for his client's welfare; just as a doctor, a lawyer, a broker does when he accepts a patient or a client. A doctor who diagnoses an illness and refuses to treat it in the hope it will go away by itself is unethical. A mechanic who refuses to tell a customer that his car's brakes are shot is unethical. A lawyer who withholds information that may stave off his client's ruin is unethical. Is it possible that the astrologer who preaches only sweetness and light is also unethical?

Since when is blindness a virtue, or ignorance a boon to humanity? Since when is it wrong to try to save a life? The human condition is perilous: no doubt it was meant to be. It is perilous because we cannot wish the world around us away by taking no notice of it, and to pretend we can merely increases our peril.

I ask you to study these charts of the Titanic disaster with care.

I wonder how many of the 1,500 people who went down with her while singing "Nearer My God to Thee" would have felt that an astrologer who warned them not to sail on that ship was being "negative."

16

Multiple Questions

Chart 9 is a multiple horary, given as an assignment to a class of students, who were told to write down a question at that moment. They were then told to exchange their questions with other class members, who were to answer the question asked and bring the results to the next session.

A young married woman with several small children asked, "Will I have to go to work before the end of the year?"

The answer was yes, probably in about six months, when the sign on the MC (career, status) changed from Pisces to Aries and began to form the opposition to Pluto at the Nadir. The reason she would have to go to work was shown to be the break-up of her marriage: Uranus (divorce) in her fourth house (home) opposition Mars (quarrels, incompatibility, rupture), and the seventh cusp (marriage) square Uranus. Also Saturn, ruler of the seventh, is in the last degree of Taurus and retrograde, indicating that attempts to hold the marriage together would not work out (retrograde planets do not deliver what they promise). When Saturn turned direct and moved into Gemini both parties would realize it was futile to continue together, but because the Sun was trine Saturn, they would remain on friendly terms and arrive at a settlement compatible to both. Saturn also ruled the eighth (the husband's money), and its retrograde condition at the end of a sign indicated the withdrawal of his support, or a change in how it would be administered, or in its value. If Uranus is used as ruler of the eighth, the testimony is the same. Financial need is shown by the South Node in the second house (money).

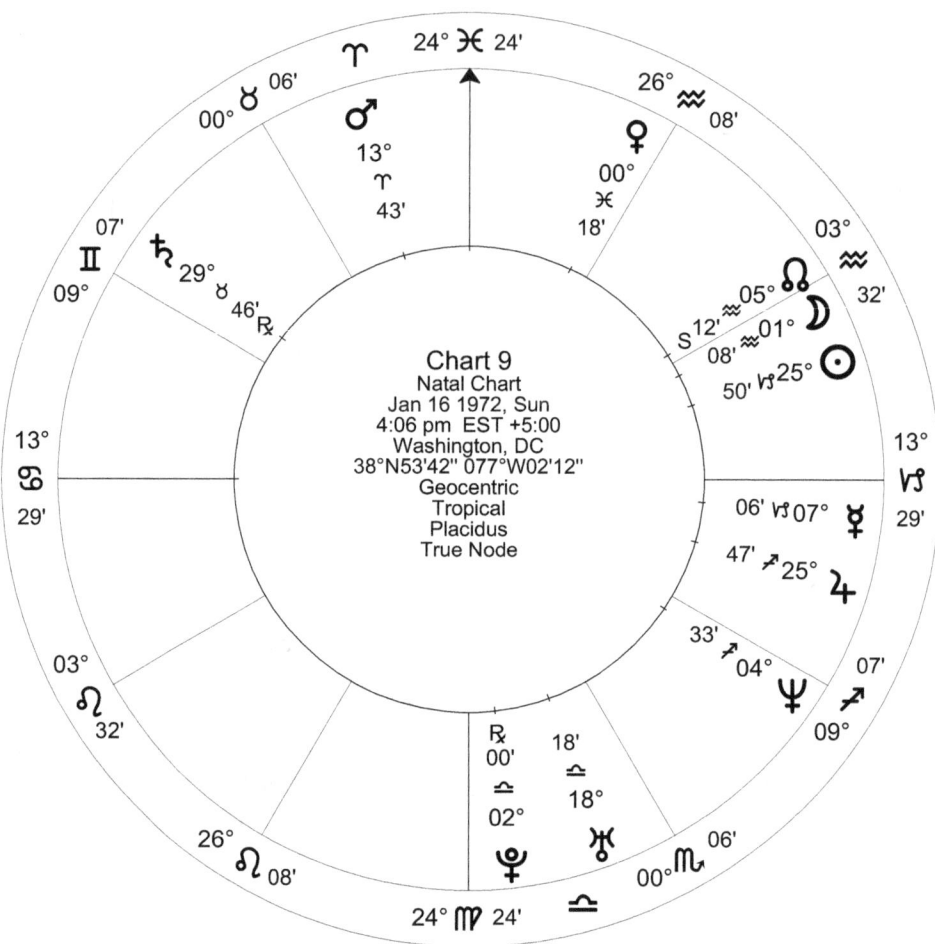

Chart 9. *Horary chart set up to answer multiple questions.*
January 16, 1972, 4:06 p.m. EST, Washington, D.C.

Employment is a sixth house matter, which usually means getting a job and working for someone else. But in this case, Jupiter, ruler of the sixth, is in its own first-house sign in the sixth; and Mars, coruler with Jupiter of the tenth (career) is also in its first-house sign in the tenth. This was a double indication of self-employment. The young woman was told that she would have to work to earn money, but that she would do this in a self-directed, professional capacity, centering the activity in her home (Mercury, ruler of the fourth, in the sixth in Capricorn, the natural tenth house sign of career). The other ruler of the fourth, Venus, was in the ninth of higher education or travel. Since travel contradicts the other indications, she was told that some of her money would come from teaching or lecturing or both. Because the Moon, ruling the querent, was in Aquarius (astrology) in the seventh house (the public) and the first aspect it makes would be a trine to Pluto (hidden resources), she was told that she would probably begin to practice astrology professionally and would teach it. Uranus (astrology) in the fourth (her home) is another indication of this. In the summer of 1972, she did begin a professional astrological practice in her home, and in the fall, she began teaching adult education courses in astrology in public high schools. A short while ago, she told me that the demand for more advanced instruction was so great that she had to organize her own classes for those who wanted to continue, and that she had rented a classroom in a church for this purpose. Pisces rules Christian churches!

Except for the unhappy feature of the broken marriage (which was not asked about directly), this chart promised a successful outcome and a constructive solution to the young woman's problem.

Chart 9 also provided the answer to an entirely different sort of question asked by another student, which was: "Should I buy a new car or get the old one repaired—if possible?"

Since automobiles are the everyday, taken-for-granted means of transportation for Americans, they are ruled by the third house and Mercury in questions Americans ask about them. In those parts of the world where automobiles are rare prestige items, accessible only to the rich and powerful, they are ruled by the ninth house and Jupiter. In using horary astrology, we must never forget this: that the placement of the question depends upon the querent's attitude toward the thing asked about. One man's necessity is another man's luxury. The horse is a sixth-house utilitarian necessity to a cowboy, but if you try to keep one in New York City, it becomes an expensive, ninth-house status symbol.

The third house of Chart 9 ruled the car the querent already had. The Sun, ruler of the third, was trine Saturn, which disposed of the Moon, ruling the querent. That the car was in bad condition, needing extensive repair, was shown by the condition of retrograde Saturn in the last degree of Taurus. The dispositor of the planet signifying the matter asked about shows the underlying condition of the thing—its basic health.

The fifth house, being the third from the third, ruled the new car the querent might buy. The fifth cusp thus became the Ascendant for the new car, and it was invalid, being less than three degrees of Scorpio. The significator of the new car was Mars in Aries, opposition Uranus, indicating a defective engine (Mars), which might cause accidents (Uranus). Neptune in the fifth on the hidden side of the sixth indicated that the querent would be defrauded of money or deluded about the value of the new car because the sixth, being the second from the fifth, showed the money involved in the purchase. Jupiter, falling in the money house of a chart concerning a purchase, or Jupiter ruling it, usually means the item costs too much and is being considered for reasons of status and prestige, rather than from necessity. That the querent could not afford the new car was indicated by his own radical second, containing the South Node, describing a vaguely unsatisfactory financial condition.

He was told not to buy a new car, but to repair the old one, which he could do at little cost if he did most of the work himself. This proved to be the case because the Sun, ruler of both his present car and his finances, was trine Saturn (necessity and work), and Saturn disposed of both the Sun and the Moon (himself).

17

Business, Finance, Investments

On January 5, 1972, at 11:30 a.m., a client called the astrologer with a problem concerning an investment in stocks. She said that a few weeks before, at a date and time she no longer remembered, she had received a letter from the company in which she held preferred stock presenting a plan to convert this to common stock on what seemed to be very favorable terms. Her broker advised her to do this, but she was reluctant. She was conservative about money and investments. She regarded preferred stock as an "investment" and common stock as a "speculation," and she was fearful of speculations. The more she thought about it, the more confused and undecided she became. Chart 10 was set up to answer her question: Shall I convert preferred stock in X Company to common?

Analysis reveals that the querent was not quite as free an agent in the matter as she supposed, because Mars and the Part of Fortune were both in the degree of the Nodes. This is always an indication of something going on that is beyond the control of the querent. The operation of unknown and uncontrollable factors behind the scenes always seems fateful to us, but of course this fatefulness may prove to be unexpectedly lucky if properly handled. In a chart containing strictures against judgment, nodal connections may indicate unexpected disaster or tragedy in an otherwise favorable chart.

In the querent's opinion, preferred stock was an investment; therefore, the second house (resources) was used to designate it. She regarded common stock as a speculation, so this was

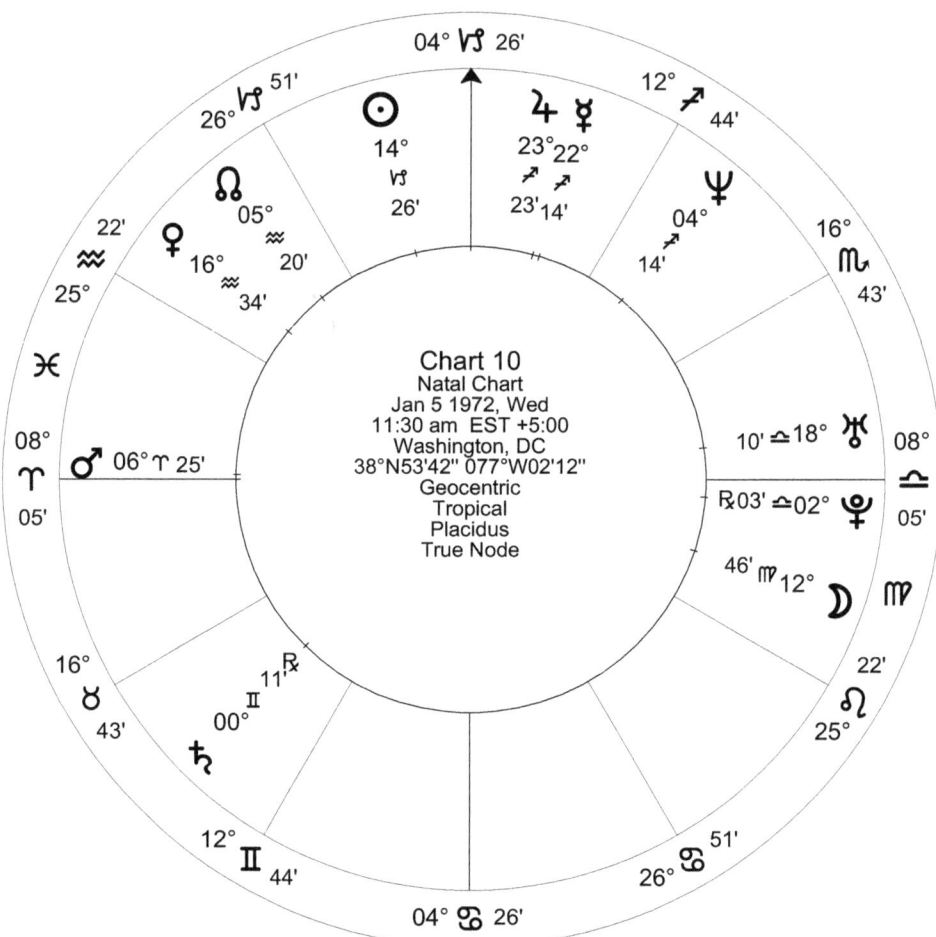

Chart 10. Question: Shall I convert preferred stock in X Company to common stock?
January 5, 1972, 11:30 a.m. EST, Washington, D.C.

placed in the fifth, which rules common stocks in any case. The querent herself was ruled by the Ascendant and Mars. The rising Mars in the degree of the Nodes and trine the Part of Fortune meant that she had to take action, whether or not she wanted to. Circumstances would not allow her to sit pat doing nothing for long. Sitting pat meant keeping the preferred stock, and the demand of the rising Mars in Aries for positive action was a testimony against doing this.

Next, the ruler of the second (preferred stock) was Venus in Aquarius trine Uranus and in mutual reception with it. Aquarius rules large corporations and Uranus rules reorganization. She was told that the company was getting rid of its preferred stock because it was planning to reorganize and perhaps become part of a larger conglomerate (Uranus). Saturn retrograde in the second, moving back into Taurus, was another indication of the same thing: the company (Saturn) was getting rid of something—namely the preferred stock. If she continued to hold it, it would decline in value and there might come a time when she could not find a ready market if she wanted to sell it.

The fifth house (common stock) had the last degree and minute of Cancer on the cusp. This meant that the old situation was all washed up. Very likely after the stock conversion was finished and the company had only one type of common stock, this would in turn be converted to something else, probably into shares of the larger company (Uranus), which was absorbing Company X in a new conglomerate. The South Node in the fifth meant that Company X's common stock was also under some type of pressure. But with Venus (ruler of the preferred stock) trine Uranus and in mutual reception with it, the way out was the transfer; with the Moon ruler of the fifth trine the Sun, the transfer was to the querent's advantage. She would be given a book value of common stock greater than the book value of the preferred because Mercury, ruler of the third house of book values, was conjunction Jupiter. The many trines between significators indicated that the very process of conversion would cause the common stock to rise within the next year and a half. If holding common stock made her nervous, she could sell it advantageously during that period.

She remarked that, although the broker had not told her all these details, his advice was the same: to convert. In the back of her mind had been an unspoken question about the broker's integrity. The sixth house and Virgo rules brokers. With the Moon there trine the Sun, the broker's advice was undoubtedly sound.

Only then did the astrologer ask what Company X produced. The answer: food products! The Moon, ruler of function is in the sixth house of commodities in Virgo, the food sign.

The next time I saw this client she told me she had made the transfer and felt very good about it because the common stock was already going up at a great rate.

Chart 11 was cast for the moment when a salesman called on me to explain the mechanics of investing in Scotch whisky. I had previously received literature about this in the mail which sounded interesting, so I had requested more information. But I had done this on impulse and had no record of the time or date. Therefore, the first legitimate chart I could cast was this one for an event: the moment the salesman called.

The Ascendant was invalid, being less than three degrees of Leo. The South Node was rising, with Venus (finances) exactly square it. The Moon (function) was 8 from an exact square to Mercury. The Sun, ruler of the second (the money I would have to invest) was in the ninth (foreign countries) in Pisces, the sign ruling whisky, but it formed no aspect to anything, having just passed a sextile to Mars and a quincunx to Uranus. This was all bad news for an investment in Scotch whisky at that time. Notice Neptune, ruler of liquor, retrograde in the fifth house of spec-

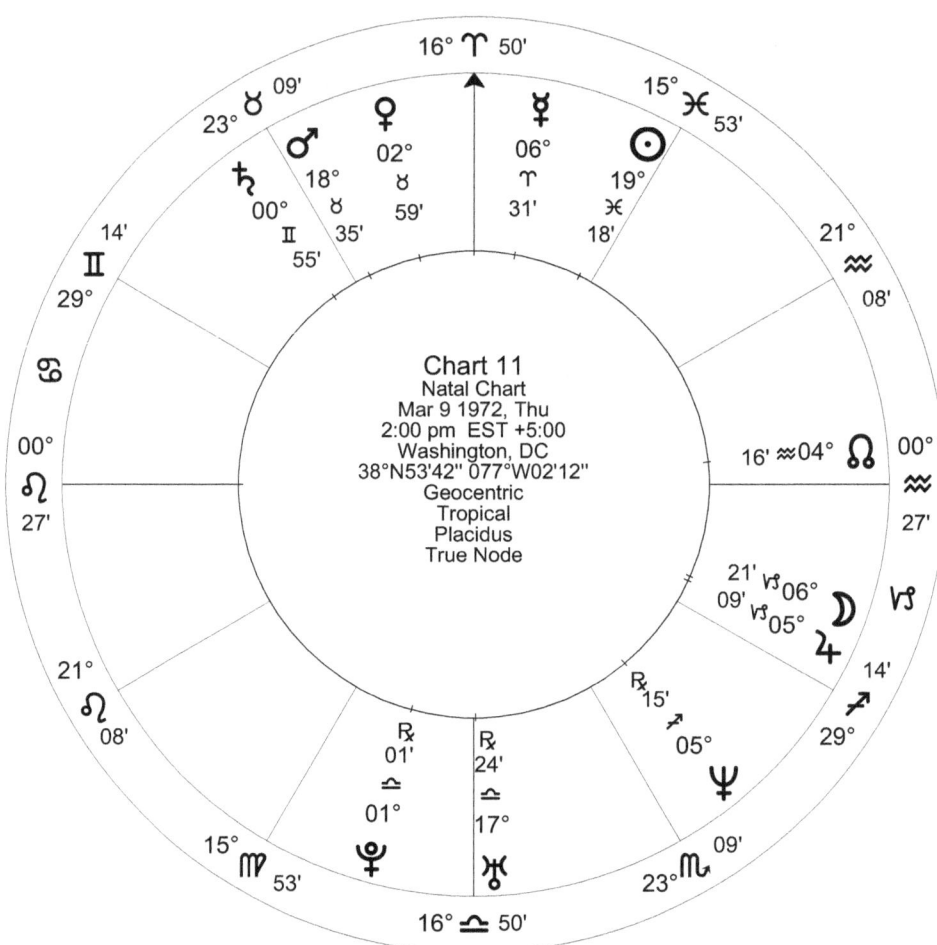

*Chart 11. Event: Salesman called to offer investment in Scotch whisky.
March 9, 1972, 2:00 p.m. EST, Washington, D.C.*

ulation, opposing Saturn (fall in price or value). The promise of profit was rosy, seemingly absolutely foolproof for large capital gains in four years when the raw whisky I bought would be mature and salable. But something was definitely wrong with the promises. Events beyond anyone's control would spoil everything. The last degree of Sagittarius on the sixth house of commodities (whisky is a commodity) indicated a coming change of status that would make a revision of the whole picture necessary. But although this was an event chart and could, therefore, be read, the strictures against judgment and the bad fatality indicated by Venus square the Nodes made it impossible to predict exactly what would happen to spoil everything and result in a loss for me.

Naturally, I did not invest in Scotch whisky. On October 25 and 26, 1972, the pound collapsed and any investment that had been made in pounds collapsed with it. Venus rules currency in this case foreign currency since it was in the second from the ninth of foreign countries. Venus in the degree of the Nodes and square them meant that the British pound would suffer a fatality that could not have been foreseen on March 9, 1972, when this chart was cast.

Chart 12 was drawn to answer a question about a business in which the querent might become involved as a cofounder and part owner of the company. Unfortunately, the querent could not remember the date and hour when the subject was first broached. But as time passed, she felt increasingly dubious about the proposition. Therefore, at 12:45 p.m. EST on January 12, 1972, in Washington, D.C., she asked the question: How will the cassette business work out for me?

The background was as follows: a public relations consultant in New York, whom we will call Miss P.R., had a number of clients with special skills, such as dressmaking, hair dressing, make-up, cooking, diet and exercise, occult subjects, and various handcrafts. Miss P.R. decided that there was considerable demand for experts to teach these fields, but that many of the people who wanted to learn lived in areas where teachers were unavailable. So Miss P.R. decided that the answer was to found a corporation that would market audio-visual equipment, probably on a rental basis, and sell courses in the various subjects to small groups of ten or twelve who could split the cost of instruction. Each individual in the group could learn at little expense, but the company would make a lot of money.

Obviously, this is not a bad idea, and given enough capital to promote it on a national scale, it might well succeed. Unfortunately, Miss P.R. had no money. She was extremely optimistic about borrowing it, however, and she put in a lot of hard work talking to manufacturers of audio-visual equipment, each of whom was suspiciously eager to offer a deal whereby Miss P.R. could get all the equipment she needed without investing a cent in it.

Miss P.R. had many connections with beauty schools, salons, and cosmetic manufacturers. She planned to start with this market, selling tapes and films of famous hairdressers and makeup artists showing students how they did it. She foresaw easy success in this field, which would immediately raise money to invest in developing and promoting instruction in other fields. The querent's special field would also be exploited early in the game, as it was very popular just then and instruction in it was hard to find, even in big cities.

As Miss P.R. planned the venture, it would be necessary to take the following people in on the ground floor as equal founders of the corporation: a photographer, a hairdresser, a cosmetician, the querent, and herself. These five would work for nothing until the business was established and the money started coming in. Then, they would share equally in the profits. The burden of raising the capital and promoting the product would be on Miss P.R. The others would simply do their own thing as necessary, each of them paying his or her personal expenses for travel and

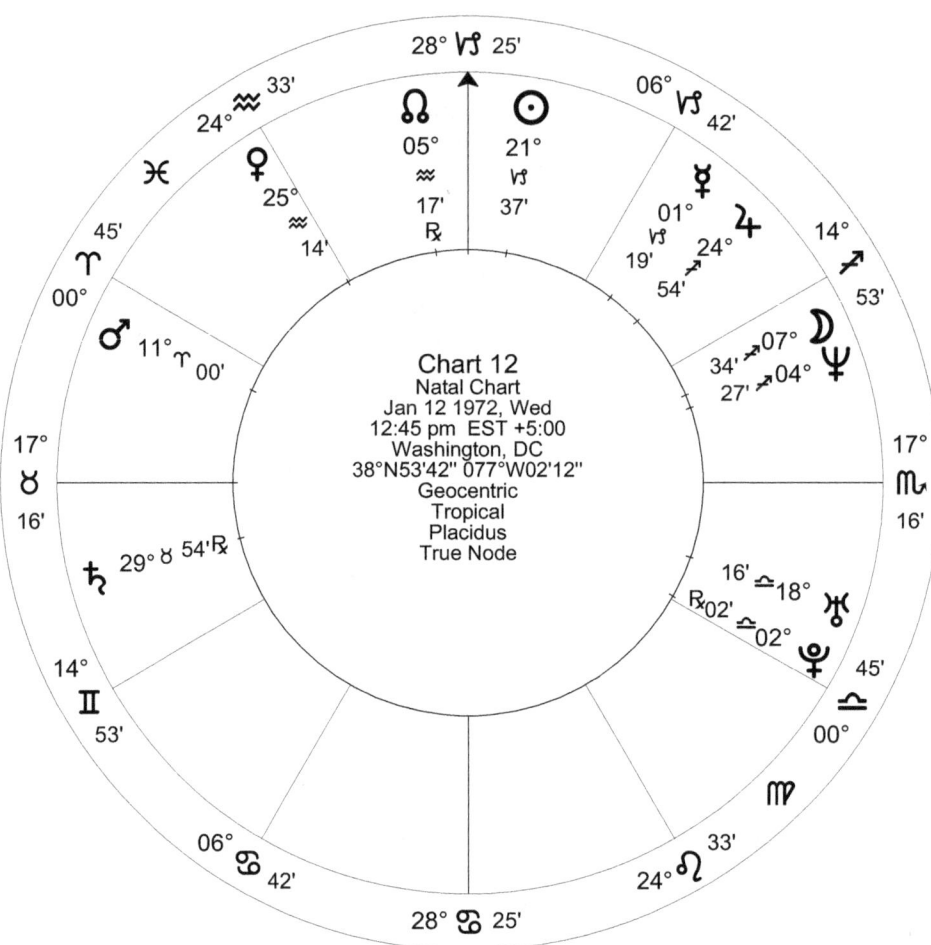

Chart 12. Question: How will the cassette business work out for me?
January 12, 1972, 12:45 p.m. EST, Washington, D.C.

equipment as the need arose. None of these people was asked to provide capital because Miss P.R. assumed that none of them had any money. This assumption was correct, except in regard to the querent, who had plenty—a good deal more, in fact, than Miss P.R. planned to borrow.

The Ascendant of Chart 12 represents the querent and describes the impression she made on others, including Miss P.R. With Taurus rising and Venus in Aquarius, she was an intellectual person who lived a quiet, unpretentious life and kept her mouth shut about her personal affairs. The retrograde Saturn rising gave a false impression of poverty. Retrograde planets always lie! Notice that Venus is in mutual reception with both Saturn and Uranus, the two rulers of Aquarius. This meant that the querent had many hidden resources undreamt of by Miss P.R.

The seventh house of partnership represented Miss P.R., who was, therefore, ruled by Mars in Aries in the twelfth, Miss P.R.'s own sixth house of work. She was indeed a tireless dynamo of energy when it came to work. But, typical of Mars in Aries, much of this energy was wasted through misdirection, fruitless running around, and inability to sit quietly and plan her campaigns. With the Moon in Sagittarius trine Mars, Miss P.R. was strongly status conscious, but the status had to show conspicuously for her to believe in it: there had to be Cadillacs at the door and a lot of name-dropping. With Jupiter in Miss P.R.'s second, she was almost pathologically money-conscious and never stopped talking about it. Since the querent seldom mentioned it, it must follow, in Miss P.R.'s book, that she was poor.

The last planet the Moon went over was Neptune, both in the seventh house. This had a double meaning because the seventh represents both Miss P.R. herself and her proposition—the new company. The querent was told that Miss P.R. was basically dishonest (Neptune) and addicted to promising everyone, including herself, pie in the sky. The company might well be a delusion (Neptune); but if it ever did get founded, its operations would be shady and its foundations wobbly. The midpoint of Neptune and Jupiter was 14 Sagittarius 41, falling exactly on Miss P.R.'s second cusp and on the querent's eighth of loss. Jupiter-Neptune midpoints or conjunctions are indicators of embezzlement. Therefore, it seemed likely that if this company ever did get started, Miss P.R. might embezzle some of its funds.

The querent's second house of money was ruled by Mercury falling in her eighth of loss, square Pluto, coruler of Miss P.R.

Audiovisual education is ruled by the third and ninth houses: the third rules the appliance and the ninth the instruction given with it. The third is in good condition with its ruler trine Mars, indicating that Miss P.R. would certainly be able to get all the appliances she needed and on a favorable basis. But the ninth, ruled by the retrograde Saturn rising, square Venus ruling the querent, indicated that the querent would never give any instruction in her specialty, no matter what was projected for her or promised to her. The late degree of Cancer on the fourth (final outcome) indicated that something about the project was outmoded, or too old to be viable. The querent learned later from someone conversant with the field that this was the design of the audiovisual cassettes themselves: there had been breakthroughs in design, which rendered all those that had been offered to Miss P.R. undesirable.

In any case, the querent was told that the business would work out very badly for her, regardless of what the others involved did. She was advised to withdraw from the whole thing as unobtrusively as possible before she invested either time or money in it. She did this with considerable relief, for, she said, the chart exactly described her doubts and fears about the whole project.

18

Missing People

Chart 13 was drawn regarding this concern: I just learned that a friend who is also one of my customers has disappeared. Will she be found and where? Can astrology locate her? The question was asked by a student, and the problem was given to my horary class to solve.

The woman had actually disappeared on January 13. She was twenty-nine years old, weighed 103 pounds, was five feet tall, and very pretty. She was married, had two small children, and owned an antique shop in Georgetown. She was last seen when she left her home to go to work.

Since the question was asked about a friend, the eleventh house of the radical chart was made the Ascendant of the judgment chart. With 28 Aries 40 on this cusp, we immediately see that the question was asked too late: the matter is hopeless. With Jupiter, ruler of her twelfth of misfortune and her eighth of death in the degree of the Nodes, we suspect that she suffered some fatality. With Venus, coruler of the judgment Ascendant also in her twelfth, she was either imprisoned or dead, probably the latter because of the close opposition of Venus to the retrograde Uranus, coruler of her tenth, the house of fate.

Mars, ruler of the judgment Ascendant (her physical body), was intercepted in the first house in Taurus in a violent degree. She was physically assaulted, probably raped. Mars was in mutual reception with Venus, from which we concluded that her body has been moved from the place where she was killed and hidden elsewhere. Mars and Venus are also corulers of her seventh

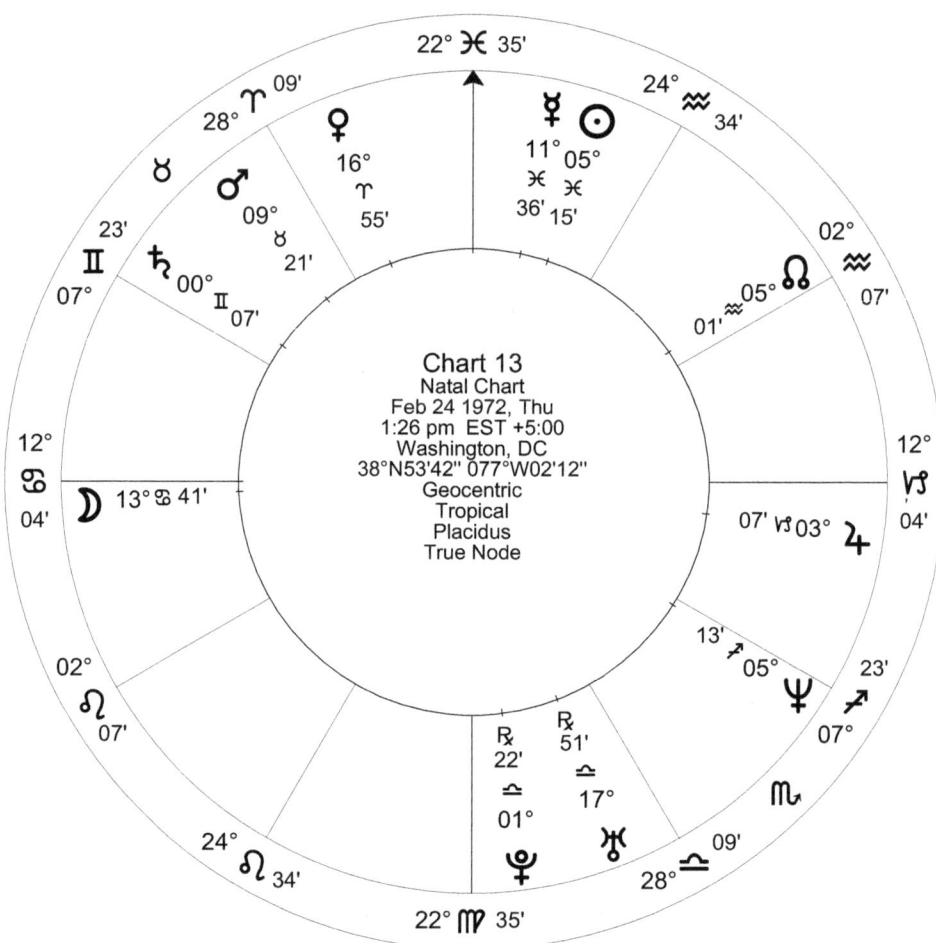

Chart 13. Question: I just learned a friend has disappeared. Will she be found and where?
February 24, 1972, 1:26 p.m.

house of open enemies, of attack, and of criminals at large. There might have been two killer-rapists. This is further borne out by both Mars and Saturn in the judgment Ascendant. One of them threatened her with a gun or knife (Mars), while the other bound (Saturn) her hands and arms (Gemini). But the actual cause of death was probably suffocation (Saturn in Gemini opposition Neptune), so judged because the last planet the Moon passed over was Saturn. Mars in Taurus is associated with violent injury to the neck or throat.

Her killers were probably black men with criminal records because Neptune was in the judgment seventh of criminals-at-large but on the hidden side of the judgment eighth (death, agents of death). And the Sun, ruler of the judgment fourth (end of life) was but two minutes past an exact square to Neptune. Probably the killing was accidental and only rape had been intended because Venus was opposition the retrograde Uranus (unexpected accidents). Retrograde planets upset plans.

In charts of this type, the Moon always signifies the missing person or thing. One of the oldest aphorisms of horary astrology says that when the Moon is rising in the radical Ascendant and applying to a retrograde planet, the missing person or thing will be found, though not in good condition if the Moon is badly afflicted. Here, it was applying to both Venus and Uranus in square aspects: she would be found dead.

Where? In or near running water, a canal or river (Cancer) in her own neighborhood (Georgetown), because the Moon was in the judgment third house of everyday environment. When? In about four months, when the Moon by horary timing reached the midpoint of Venus-Uranus, which was 17 Cancer 24.

Her body was actually found in the Potomac near a boat house in Georgetown, in May. This was four months from the time of her disappearance, but only three from the time the question was asked. William Lilly, the great master of horary art, felt that time judgments should be shortened when all the applications were in cardinal signs and angles, as here. Also, when the Moon applies to a retrograde planet, both bodies are moving toward each other, and the time may, therefore, be speeded up. But I have found many other cases like this, where the time estimate tallies closely with the disappearance of the person or object, although the question about it was asked much later.

The police released the notice to the press that the woman's body was found, and where, but no further details have been printed. The student who asked the question tried to get more information from a friend in the police department, but was told that the case was still under investigation. Even information from the coroner's report about the condition of the body could not be revealed. He learned from another source, however, that the police did have a suspect under surveillance. I would judge from the retrograde Pluto (mystery) in the fourth (end of the matter) of the radical chart, trine Saturn, ruler of the radical seventh (criminal at large) that they are watching the wrong man, and that the actual killers will not be arrested. Or, if they are, it will be in connection with another crime.

19

Health

Health is one of the great preoccupations of people who ask questions of astrologers. The practitioner soon comes to feel that we are a nation of hypochondriacs, a conclusion readily supported by the stream of advertising pushing pills and miracle cures for every human ill. An evening with the tube exposes us to a procession of actors graphically portraying physical misery and the terrible dangers we are exposed to from malnutrition, germs in the toilet bowl, the smells generated by our bodies, and failure to eat the right cereal or fruit juice.

Perhaps this obscene preoccupation with our stomachs, nerves, and intestinal tracts is merely a negative expression of our national chart. We have four planets in Cancer, a hypochondriacal sign, with the Sun (vitality) square Saturn (gloom); Mercury (nerves) opposition Pluto (bowels and noxious smells); Mars (energy) square Neptune (drugs, poisons, synthetics, and delusions) in Virgo, the food and drug sign. The astrologer, like the physician and the psychiatrist, is constantly exposed to the backlash of this unwholesome will to be ill. With experience, each of us develops his or her personal technique for handling these demands for astrological miracle cures for nonexistent ailments. But we must not allow our impatience with the hypochondriac, who pesters both his astrologer and his doctor, to obscure our recognition of real illness when we see it.

Most of us are seriously ill at some time in our lives. Some people are accident prone, and even those who are not may have accidents at certain times. Some people suffer from genetic defects that make them victims of a variety of serious diseases. Some people were born with a general lack of vitality resulting in an inability to throw off infection. Some people have been left permanently crippled by diseases like osteomyelitis or poliomyelitis, by accidents, or wounds. The astrologer must try to learn the patterns of real illness in the natal chart and to treat them with respect. This is not easy because medical astrology is a still unborn science. Most of the information we have about it comes down to us from the middle ages and is worth very little. In fact, by glibly repeating medieval lore that we read in some book, we may unwittingly do a client great harm.

Remember that unless the astrologer is also a physician, he is not qualified to practice medicine. It is against the law to do so. The day will surely come when we can work openly with the medical profession. In the meantime, we can increase our knowledge in this field if all of us try to keep track of our clients who are seriously ill, keep notes on the physician's diagnosis, the treatment administered, and the results obtained. Careful comparisons of these facts with the natal charts may eventually lead to greater understanding of the astrological patterns associated with certain physical conditions, and possibly the mental and emotional temperaments that encourage some diseases and inhibit others.

A serious disease or accident is never simple, astrologically. It shows in the chart as a complex of many factors. Some of them, like antiscion degrees and midpoints, are quite subtle. The aspects involved are by no means always bad. Trines and sextiles predominate in the charts of many schizophrenics, congenital idiots, dipsomaniacs, and drug addicts. Benefic planets are involved as often as malefics, for they too have their gamut of ills. In medical astrology, the grand trine is not a blessing, for it frequently indicates an overemphasis upon one element an excess of something that results in lack of balance both in the chart and in the body.

Above all, we should remember that death is often a blessed release to the very old, the chronically ill, and the permanently maimed. When this is the case, it commonly occurs on beautiful aspects: close trines from transit and solar arc Jupiter, Saturn, Uranus, and Pluto. Probably nothing we do can prevent a *timely* death. I believe, however, that there are *untimely* deaths, and that these are generally shown by heavy, malefic stress over the natal chart, bringing out the worst in it. When we see such heavy stress, we should not take chances with our clients' lives by being cheerfully overoptimistic, although, we should not needlessly alarm them either. We should warn against accidents or untimely surgery during such periods, and we should try to get the client to consult a doctor without delay.

Never attempt to describe the *querent's* illness from a horary chart. If he asks, "I'm scheduled for an operation on such and such a day. Is this a good time for the surgery?" you can answer provided he names the specific condition. A good time for a bone operation might be bad for an eye operation. If the answer is, "No, you should postpone it to a better time," you must refer to the natal chart to find a more favorable day. In general, I think we should refuse to select specific dates for operations for our clients. To do so involves long hours of labor for which we are seldom adequately paid; and the responsibility is too great to be borne by people whose medical knowledge is inadequate and who have no control whatever over the competence of the surgeon or of the hospital staff. Most of us do select surgical dates, however, for ourselves and members of our immediate families.

When it is necessary to do this, we should avoid all days and hours when any of the horary strictures against judgment prevail. Never have an operation when the Moon is void-of-course, in the Via Combusta, when the Ascendant is invalid, or when Saturn is either rising or in the seventh house. Try to avoid close quincunxes from heavy planets, especially to the Moon or Ascendant during the course of the operation. Avoid planets in the degree of the Nodes. Never have an operation when Mercury is retrograde, or when the significator of the part of the body to be operated on is retrograde. Try to select a time when a benefic is angular and when the aspects the Moon forms during the surgery and immediately after it are favorable. The most ancient aphorisms concerning surgery are: Never undergo it when Mars is in Scorpio, the sign of the butcher, or when the Moon is there. Never have an operation when the Moon is in the sign ruling the part of the body in question; nor when Saturn afflicts the Moon. To this I would add, be careful of afflictions from Neptune to the Moon or the natal Ascendant: they generally indicate a bad reaction to the anesthetic.

If the querent asks about someone else's health, it is frequently possible to see the cause of the illness in the horary chart: whether it is a broken bone (Saturn-Mars), heart disease (Sun-Leo afflictions), respiratory disease (Mercury), an injury to the head (Mars-Aries), and so on. We can seldom be more specific than this, however, nor can we recommend a cure, although the success or failure of the measures the doctor takes will often show clearly in the horary chart.

Horary and event charts for surgery, or for entering a hospital, often look much worse than they actually are. This is because no one can undergo surgery or be seriously ill without traumatic aspects over his natal chart; and this trauma will inevitably show up in the horary chart if that chart is a valid description of the event. An operation is a violent assault upon the physical body. The necessity for this physical maiming is always shown by hard malefic aspects over the natal chart or in the horary. If no such traumatic aspects are present you can be quite sure the operation is not necessary and probably will not occur.

In the Middle Ages and Renaissance, when astrology and medicine were closely allied arts, one of the most important branches of horary astrology was the judgment of *decumbiture* charts, drawn for the exact moment when a sick person took to his bed. From these charts the physician and astrologer diagnosed the disease, determined the best treatment, judged when crises for better or worse would occur, and whether the patient would live or die. Long treatises were written on the art of judging such charts. The most valuable book in my library is one of these. It was written by the noted Italian mathematician, Andreas Argolus, and published in 1652, in Latin. It

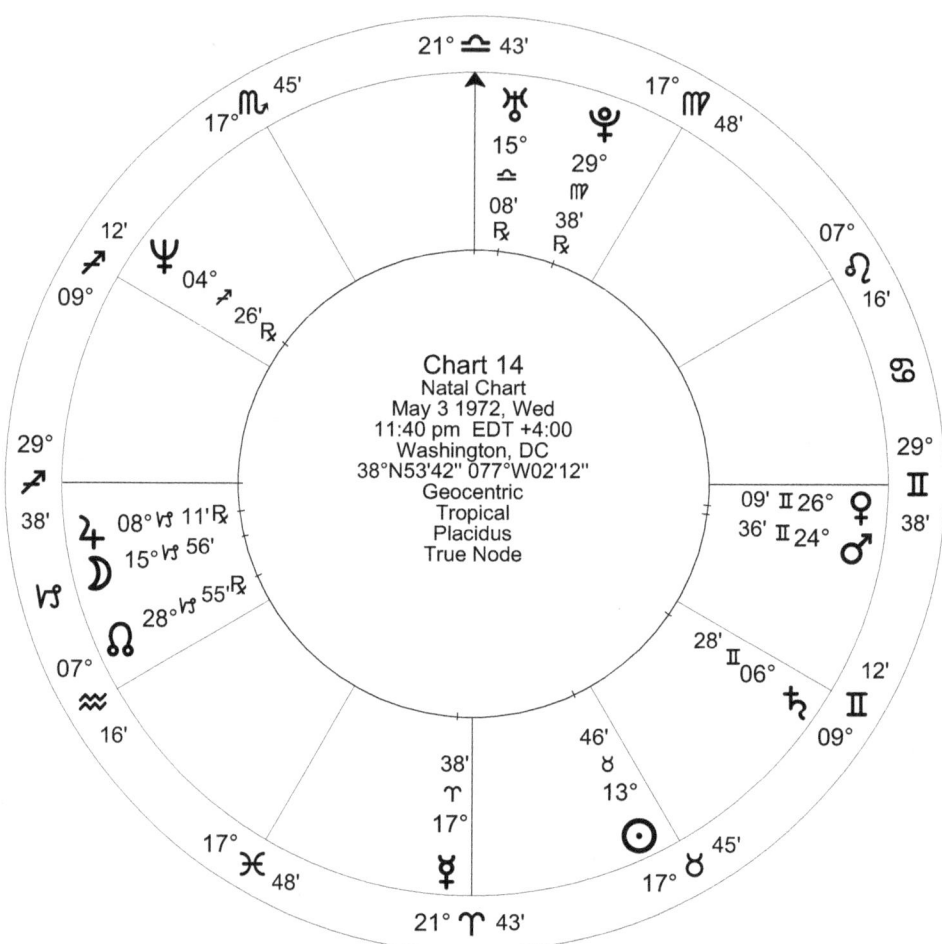

Chart 14. Event: Hospital entry of man in diabetic coma.
May 3, 1972, 11:40 p.m. EDT, Washington, D.C.

is called *De Diebus Criticis et Decubitu Aegrorum*, which means "Concerning Critical Days and the Decumbiture of the Sick." It contains dozens of charts for the decumbiture of prominent people of the Renaissance, and I judge from reading it that Argolus, like ourselves, relied heavily on natal charts if he could get them.

Chart 14 is a modern decumbiture chart, drawn for the moment when a man was admitted to a hospital in a diabetic coma.

If you want a sample of the utter confusion that surrounds medical astrology, read Cornell's definition of diabetes in his *Encyclopedia of Medical Astrology*. This work was first published in

1933, almost ten years after the cause of the disease had been discovered and the treatment by insulin injections had been established. Yet Cornell defines it as "an autosuggestive psychosis." He assigns every planet (except Pluto) some measure of involvement with it, which would make it impossible to decide from any natal chart whether a person would fall victim to it.

Diabetes is a disease of the pancreas, an endocrine gland, which results in the inability to metabolize sugar. The tendency to the disease is probably of genetic origin. There is no cure. Mild cases can be controlled by diet and pills taken orally. Severe cases are always fatal unless the patient has regular injections of insulin, a hormone manufactured by the pancreas.

All the endocrine glands manufacture hormones, which are *chemicals* that control the metabolic processes of the body. These glands form an integrated system, so that severe disturbance in one often leads to disturbances in others. The inability to metabolize something we ingest, which is vital to life, results in chemical poisoning of the whole body. Because the endocrine glands manufacture chemicals necessary for metabolism (a chemical process) and their failure to function results in poisons, I place the rulership of the whole endocrine system under Neptune, which rules chemistry, metabolism, and poison. Notice in this decumbiture chart that the retrograde Neptune has recently undergone a long opposition from Saturn, which was two degrees past when the man entered the hospital, indicating a chronic condition of long standing.

Cornell says that the signs Cancer and Virgo rule the pancreas because it is located in the abdomen. By analogy, he gives the planetary rulership to the Moon and Mercury. In my experience with diabetic charts, this does not work. Jupiter seems to rule the pancreas, though to be absolutely sure we would need to analyze thousands of charts. Venus is involved because it rules sugar. Cornell implicates the Venus-ruled sign Libra, but I find emphasis on Taurus more common. Caution in judgment is indicated here because serious cases usually show up at a comparatively early age. Many of the charts we can get to study will have Neptune in Libra, where it was for fourteen years. Probably there is no higher percentage of diabetes in that generation than in any other. The Moon is involved because it rules function. Saturn is involved because it rules the *principle of limitation*, as well as the ability to use anything productively. In any disease, like diabetes or cancer, where uncontrolled overproduction of something is the key to analysis, Jupiter (growth) and Saturn (limitation) are not functioning properly. Of course Saturn, as an anaretic, or death-dealing planet, may afflict in any serious illness without necessarily being involved in the disease syndrome itself.

In cases of diabetes and cancer, there is often too much Jupiter for Saturn to cope with. One indication of too much is a close, usually favorable, connection between Jupiter and the Moon. The Moon controls the tides of life, and the bigger the tides, the more she seems to delight in making them move. Whenever we see so great an excess of anything that it results in *malfunction,* look for conjunctions or trines of the Moon to the producing planet while the Moon at the same time receives afflictions from one or more other planets.

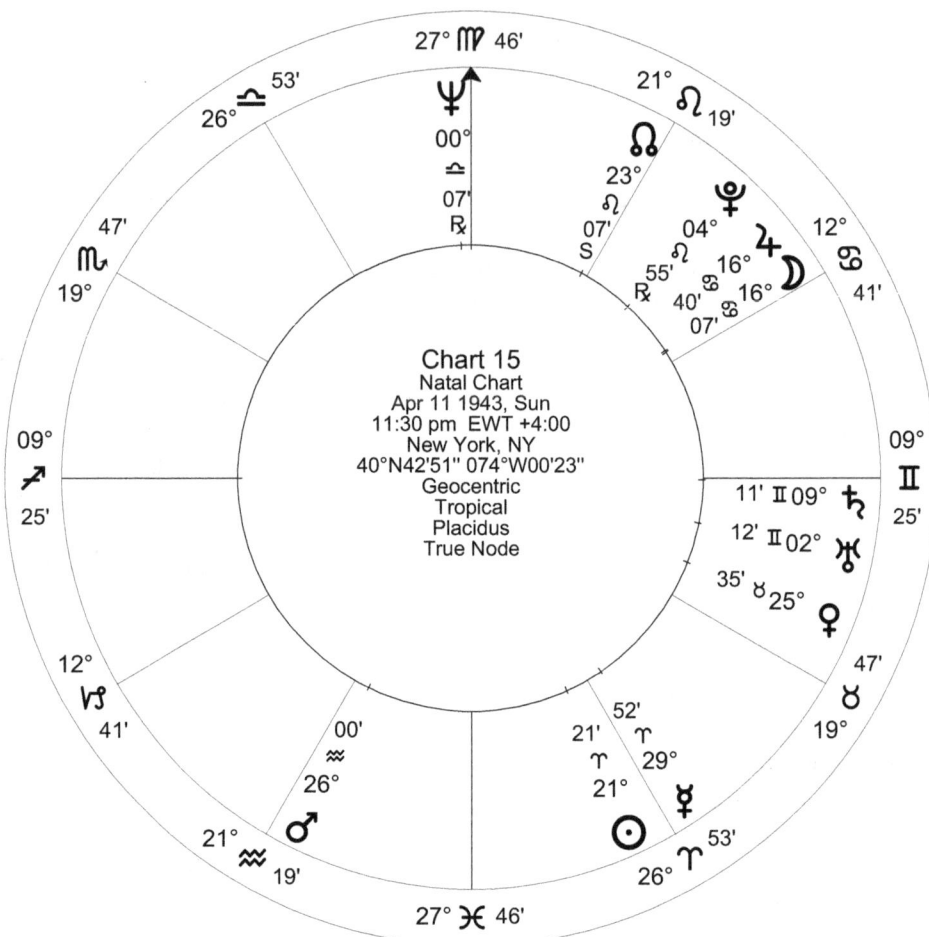

Chart 15. Natal horoscope of diabetic male. April 11, 1943, 11:30 p.m. EWT, New York City.

In this decumbiture chart, the last planet the Moon went over was the rising, retrograde Jupiter, intercepted in the Ascendant in Capricorn, applying to a quincunx to Saturn. This is a malfunctioning Jupiter. Since it is rising and the Moon last went over it, it is the key to diagnosis of the disease. The Moon is two degrees past the square to Uranus and applying to a square to Mercury.

Notice how many aspects in this chart are past by two degrees: the Moon from square to Uranus, Saturn from opposition to Neptune, Mercury from opposition to Uranus, Venus from conjunction to Mars, the sixth cusp (health) from conjunction to Saturn, Venus from opposition to the Ascendant. From this we can conclude that the patient did something two days or two hours earlier that brought on the attack. (He got drunk.)

The prognosis from this decumbiture chart is not good, although we can safely say he would not die in the hospital because the rulers of the eighth, fourth, and twelfth are not seriously enough afflicted to indicate immediate death. With an invalid Ascendant, he came to the hospital too late, with a disease of too long standing, for them to do more than pull him out of the coma. He would presumably leave when the Ascendant passed 3 Capricorn, but he would be back, either to that hospital or another for the same cause (retrograde Jupiter in the Ascendant).

This man's natal chart is number 15, given here so that you can see how the decumbiture—his transits at the time—meshes with it. Notice in the natal chart the close conjunction of the Moon and Jupiter in the eighth; the afflicted Venus in Taurus, on Algol, square Mars; Mercury quincunx Neptune (fatality through lack of judgment); Saturn opposing the Jupiter-ruled Ascendant; the Part of Fortune on Fomalhaut (genetic defects) quincunx Pluto (inheritance). The death point in this chart is 8 Scorpio 29. It is arrived at by adding the longitudes of Mars and Saturn and subtracting the longitude of the MC. I am indebted to Charles Emerson for telling me about this planetary picture, which differs from the one usually found as the Part of Death in most books. I find this one works better. Notice it is not afflicted in the decumbiture chart.

These two charts were brought to my horary class by a student who wanted to know what this man could do to lengthen his life and improve his health. He is an artist and photographer by profession. He refuses to stick to his diabetic diet, is careless about taking his insulin injections, drinks too much at times, experiments with psychedelic drugs, and generally seems bent on killing himself.

She was told to advise him to move to an area where Jupiter and the Moon would fall in the seventh and Saturn would fall in the fifth. This meant moving east by a whole time zone, into the Atlantic Ocean. Fortunately, there are plenty of West Indian islands that would do. When she told him this, and worked out a new location for him, he said he would think about it. We hope that with Neptune about to cross his Ascendant, he will not hesitate too long.

20

Legal Problems

Chart 16 is drawn for an event on November 19, 1968, at 10:48 a.m. MST, when an explosion occurred in the lavatory of a plane over Gunnison, Colorado. The plane landed safely in Denver and no one was hurt, but the last person who had visited the lavatory was immediately arrested and accused of deliberately causing the explosion. Although no trace of a bomb or other explosives was found and no motive for the act could be discovered, the man (who continued to plead his innocence) was tried and convicted.

His lawyer appealed after establishing the fact that the airline was using inferior chemicals in the toilet, chemicals which, because of their flammability, were forbidden by law. The lawyer, whom we will call Miss X., had little hope of winning the appeal, although she was convinced of her client's innocence. He was an ordinary, respectable, small business man, a foreigner, and his means were limited. The airline was powerful, rich, and influential. Nevertheless, Miss X. intended to carry the case to the Supreme Court if she had to. She was certain that there was something mysterious and hidden about the case—some small fact, which, if it could be uncovered, would free her client.

Through a chain of circumstances too complex to describe here, one of my students, Svetlana Godillo, was consulted in the matter. Working with the man's natal chart (#17), she came to the conclusion that his health was somehow involved. But, was he mentally ill, the sort who would deliberately cause an explosion through some irrational impulse; or was he physically ill, and if

138/Horary Astrology and the Judgment of Events

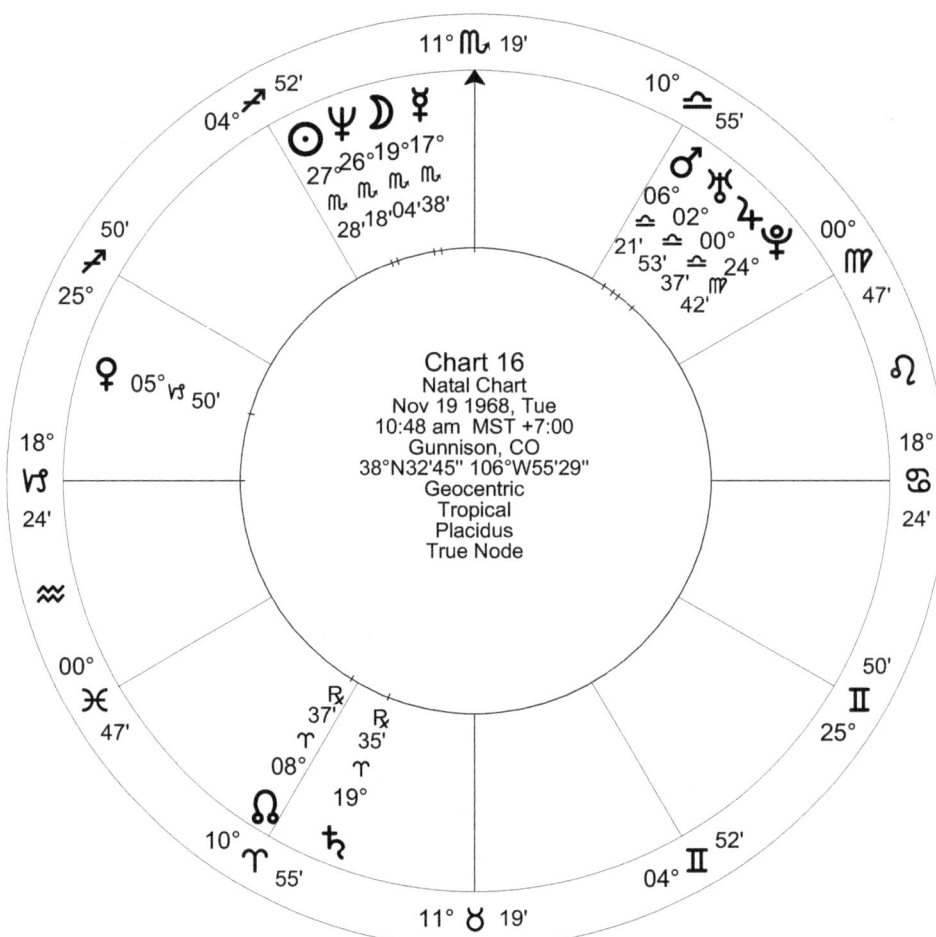

Chart 16. Event: Explosion in lavatory plane.
November 19, 1968, 10:48 a.m. MST, Gunnison, Colorado.

so, what sort of physical illness could cause an explosion when this man's urine mixed with the chemicals in the plane's toilet?

The horary chart for the event was constructed to try to resolve this question. Even if the horary chart reveals that a psychotic person is involved in the event, it must be interpreted on a factual level. The psychotic who commits a crime shows in the chart as an enemy of society or of the person he attacks. It is what he *does* that matters, not his mental condition when he did it. This may become an important fact in his defense, like an alibi or fingerprints; or a psychotic may work against him. But the astrologer cannot use it as an excuse to give a subjective interpretation of a horary chart. Horary astrology is the art of interpreting what shows on the surface or

Legal Problems/139

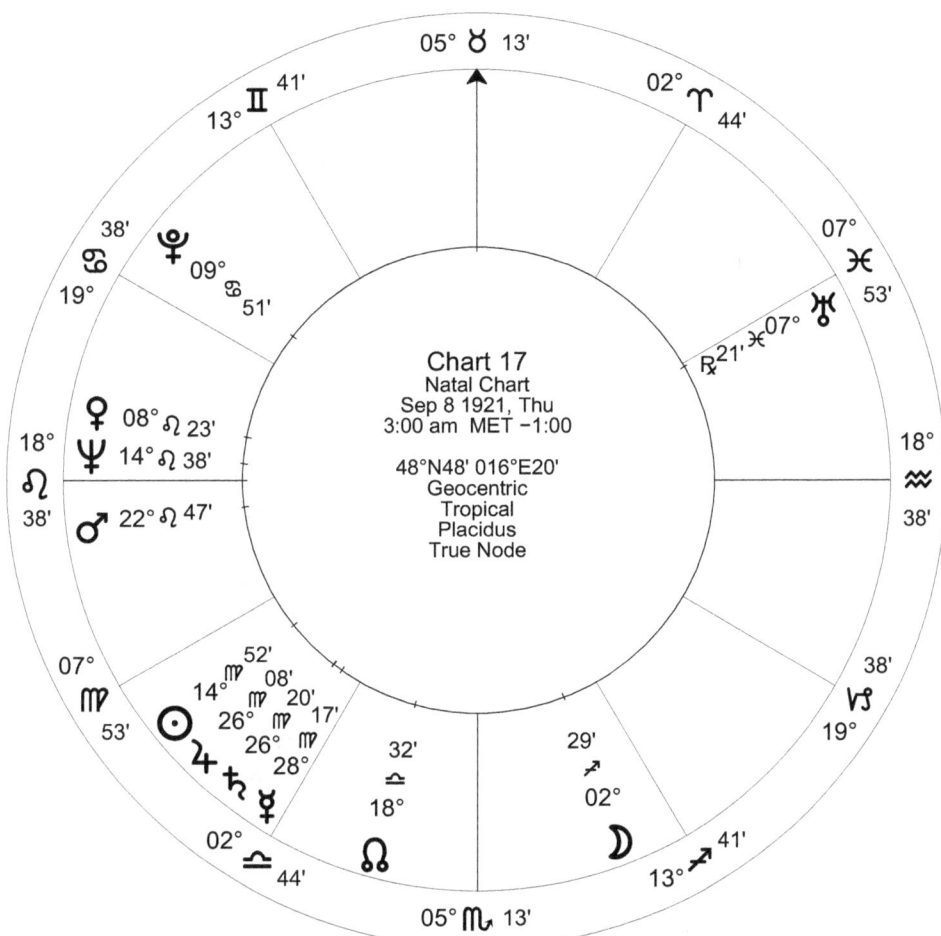

Chart 17. Natal horoscope of man arrested for causing explosion.
September 8, 1921, 3:00 a.m. MET, Lat. 48N48, Long. 16E20.

what can be brought to the surface. It concerns the material, the factual, the physical, the mundane, and the objective. Any attempt to place it in the realm of fantasy, wishes, idealism, or hidden psychological compulsions will result in failure. In horary astrology, things happen *as they happen:* what lies in the murky depths beyond them cannot be discovered from the chart.

In this case, even if the accused were mentally ill, the fact was irrelevant because it could not be used in his defense. He had no history of it, and there was no evidence in the plane or on his person when he was searched that he had used any infernal machine to cause the explosion.

Since this is an event chart, it can be considered from several points of view. We can analyze it from the point of view of Miss X., the lawyer who was convinced of her client's innocence and first sought astrological help. In this case, the ninth house, which rules lawyers, would become the judgment Ascendant. The rulerships assigned to the various houses would then be as follows:

The fourth from the ninth (radical twelfth) would rule the verdict, or final outcome. Venus, ruling Miss X., is in her fourth, indicating that the verdict would be brought about through her efforts, and might be favorable because Venus is a benefic. It is badly afflicted, however, having passed over squares to Jupiter and Uranus (the unfavorable verdict in the first trial), and is facing another square to Mars, which could bring another unfavorable verdict from the Appeals Court. The two verdicts are shown by the late degree of Sagittarius on her fourth and Venus in that house, but in a different sign. Despite its immediate afflictions, this Venus is stronger than it seems on the surface because it disposes of Jupiter, Uranus, and Mars, and through its disposition of Mars, it eventually disposes of Saturn. This puts it in triple reception with Saturn. Aspects operate on the surface, and, if they are bad, they show up immediately as adverse circumstances. Disposition operates below the surface and describes underlying conditions that have a bearing on the case. In a natal chart, these underlying conditions would be rooted in the native's character. In a horary chart, they pertain to basic facts. In this case, these facts were hidden from the public view because the Venus falls in the twelfth (secrets) of the radical chart.

The sixth from the ninth (radical second) would rule Miss X.'s client, the accused. Jupiter and Neptune are corulers of this house (again, two trials), and there is an invalid degree on the cusp, which is close quincunx Jupiter, showing the unfavorable verdict in the first trial. Notice the Jupiter in the radical eighth (latrines), and Neptune in Scorpio, the natural eighth sign (latrines). Jupiter is also the ruler of the natural ninth sign (travel) and Neptune is in the accused's ninth house (travel). Less than 3 degrees on a cusp shows *immaturity* or overhasty action. The circumstances ruled by that house collapse because action pertaining to them was ill considered and poorly planned. This looks favorable for the accused because it indicates a change in his status, which could happen only if the verdict against him was set aside by the appeals court. The North Node here, in the degree of Mars, shows how dangerous and fateful his situation was. The fatality shown by these nodal connections is generally accidental, not the person's fault. They are Karmic: he happens to be in the wrong place at the wrong time, and is caught up in a net of fateful circumstances over which he has no control. This is an argument for the innocence of the accused, but it is not an indication that he could necessarily avoid imprisonment.

The seventh from the ninth, (the radical 3third), would rule Miss X.'s adversaries in court: the prosecution. The retrograde Saturn here means they will eventually lose their case, and is another indication of two trials: what a retrograde planet does initially must be done over, and what it promises initially will be reversed. The prosecution won the first trial, but they would not win the appeal. Mars ruling this house and conjunction the South Node also indicates their defeat.

The fourth from her sixth (the radical fifth) rules the final outcome for the accused. Gemini here is another indication of two trials, turning in different verdicts. The ruler, Mercury, is in mutual reception with Pluto: there is a way out through the exposure of hidden knowledge (Pluto) which exists in documents or papers (Mercury).

The Court, from Miss X.'s viewpoint, is ruled by the tenth from the ninth (the radical sixth) and it gives the same testimony as the previous house, the final outcome for the accused. But here we have additional testimony because a late degree of Gemini is on the cusp, indicating that different conditions would prevail at the second trial. This cusp is quincunx Neptune, ruling the accused, and the Sun, testimony that new information would be of a fateful or tragic nature for the accused and would be something concerning his health because this is a sixth house quincunx.

The health of the accused is ruled by the sixth from the second (the radical seventh). The Moon, ruling the degree on the cusp, last passed over Mercury in Scorpio, indicating that the health problem is of long standing (fixed signs) and in some way involves malfunctioning of the excretory organs (Scorpio) because the Moon is quincunx Saturn and the cusp is square it. Because the Moon is applying to a conjunction with Neptune, chemicals, drugs, and even poisons cannot be ruled out as decisive factors in the case. The connections of the seventh house and its ruler with Saturn say that the disease is a very serious one, but, because the cusp is trine the Moon, it is under control. Eventually, the Moon will make a conjunction with the Sun, the other seventh ruler. This new Moon coming up indicates a new day dawning for the accused, the start of a new phase in his life. But this depends entirely upon revelations about his health coming out in court. If he were convicted and sent to prison, it would also be a new phase.

On the basis of all this, Miss X. was advised to get all the documents relating to her client's health and medical history. She was told that he was suffering from a disease that would be fatal if it were not controlled by drugs; that it was probably a disease involving the endocrine gland system (Neptune) and glands or hormones ruled by Jupiter and Venus. The accused was in fact living on borrowed time and the grace of medicine, shown by Mars in the degree of the Nodes and Pluto (death) in the radical eighth in mutual reception with the eighth ruler.

Miss X. did this and found that the accused suffered from a severe case of diabetes. He was kept alive by insulin injections. He excreted chemicals (Neptune) in his urine (Scorpio) that reacted with the inferior and illegal chemicals in the toilet to create the explosion. In fact, the reason the chemicals used had been ruled illegal was because there were many chemicals excreted in human urine that might cause such an explosive reaction. The appeals court dismissed the case against the accused. Proceedings were initiated against the airline for evading the law in a manner that put the lives of passengers in jeopardy.

This chart can also be read from the point of view of the prosecution. In that case, the radical first rules the prosecution; the seventh rules the defense; the tenth rules the court; and the fourth rules the verdict. The answer thus obtained will be exactly the same: the prosecution would lose their case because Saturn, their ruler, is retrograde and afflicted. They would lose because of a reversal (retrograde planets deliver the opposite of what is promised) in a higher court. The reversal would come about through additional evidence contained in documents, ruled by the third house which contains their significator, Saturn. Mercury (evidence) in the tenth (the Court) in mutual reception with the ruler of the tenth also indicates that the Court would change its mind.

Notice that bad as the aspects are in this chart, all the planets except Saturn are direct. In horary astrology, the person or party signified by a retrograde planet cannot win in any adversary proceeding such as a trial, an election, a game, a contest. Knowing this simple fact can save money and heartache for those who enjoy betting on such things.

Chart 18 represents one of the most serious problems I ever had to solve by horary astrology. It was drawn for November 3, 1965, at 7: 35 a.m. in Washington, D.C., when my client, who was about to board a bus to go to work, was accosted by a plainclothes detective and told to identify himself. When he asked why, the detective said he was suspected of breaking and entering. After further conversation, the detective consented to let my client go on to work on condition that he would report to the police station by four o'clock that afternoon. He called me at 9:30 a.m., gave me the details above, asked me to cast a chart for the event, and said he would come by immediately after he had talked to the police and knew more about the charges against him.

I cast the chart, and one thing was immediately clear: with the Moon in Pisces applying to a conjunction to Saturn, the matter was very serious indeed.

When he appeared about five o'clock he told me that a young woman had identified him as the person who had broken into her apartment at about 10:30 p.m. on the night of April 14, 1965, and made obscene advances to her. The police refused to give him any further details. He had no idea who his accuser was or where she lived.

I asked if he knew a lawyer who could defend him. He said he did not. I told him the chart indicated two lawyers would be involved; the first would be a woman who would not take the case, but would refer him to a man who would. Therefore, he should get on the phone immediately and call the first woman lawyer he could think of. She happened to be extremely prominent. By good luck she was still in her office. She listened courteously to my client, but said that she did not take criminal cases and there was no one in her firm who did. She referred him to another woman lawyer. This one was in court. While we waited for her to get back to her office and return my client's call, I began to analyze the chart.

Although this was an event, it was an intensely personal one that threatened my client's liberty, reputation, career, and entire future. I was deeply concerned because I knew, from years of working with this man's natal chart, that he was innocent. The crime he was accused of was

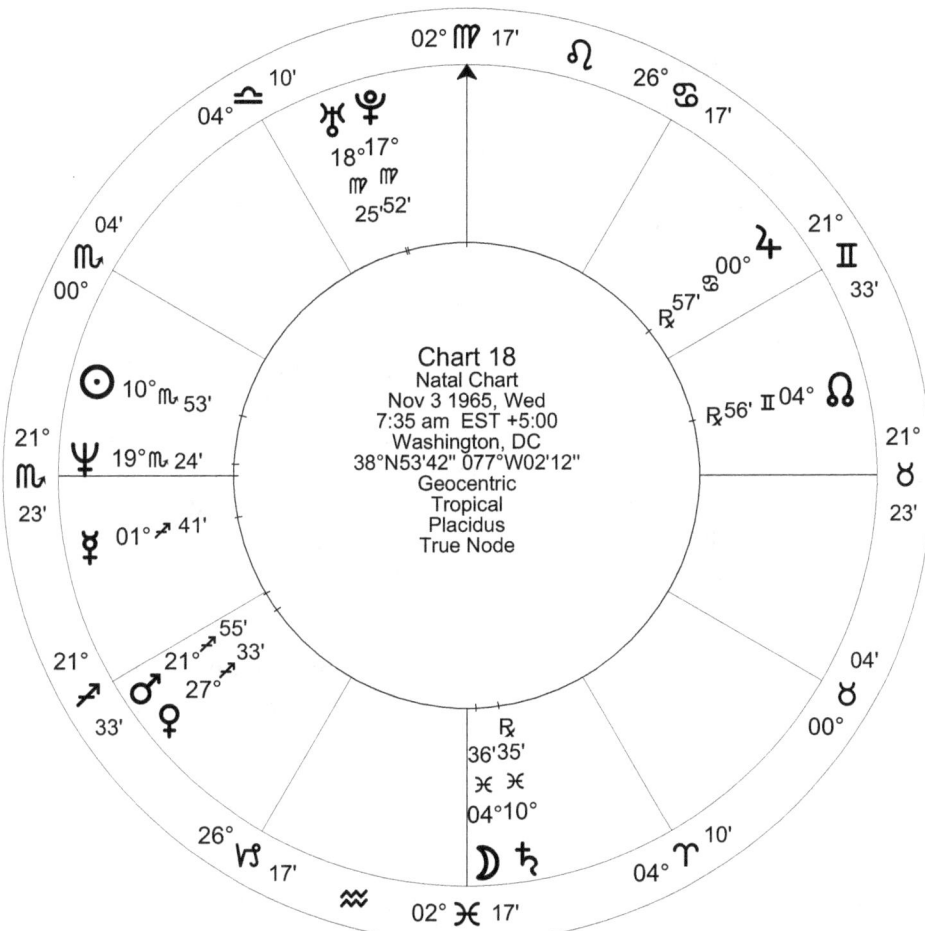

Chart 18. Event: Client arrested. November 3, 1965, 7:35 a.m. EST, Washington, D.C.

completely out of character. He was a rational, highly intelligent person, of gentle manners, unfailingly courteous, and far too normal sexually to be interested in making obscene advances to strange women. The crude kookiness and exhibitionism of this crime ruled it out, as far as he could be concerned. Besides, he was much in love at the time with a girl who took quite adequate care of him.

Unfortunately, his natal chart showed a trend toward incarceration. Given the right circumstances, he could become a prisoner of war, a concentration camp victim, a political prisoner, or he could be convicted on a false accusation, which was the possibility here. I had discussed this problem with him frankly in going over his natal chart, so that by the time of this incident he was aware that his chart had a Karmic affinity for imprisonment. He not only knew that he could not get by with any dishonest act; he also knew that he would have to learn to translate the meaning of his natal twelfth house from the obvious lowest level of Karmic fulfillment (prison or self-inflicted illness) to a higher level. Such a translation of Karma is possible only to highly developed people. It is not within the scope of this book to describe how it is done. But he was beginning to understand what was involved, and the last thing he would have risked was to jeopardize his freedom by committing a crime as silly and pointless as this one.

Because of the intense personal involvement, I decided to read the chart as a straight horary problem. The previous case could be treated as an impersonal event because the defendant's lawyer presented it. The astrologer knew neither the accused, nor whether he was innocent or guilty. Here, however, my absolute knowledge of my client's innocence made the question boil down to this: how could he best be defended against a false accusation? As a horary problem, the rulership would be: the first house, the querent, about to go on trial; the seventh, his accuser; the tenth, the Court; the fourth, the verdict. The ninth would rule his lawyers, the eleventh the jury. The second would rule his resources (I told him his defense would cost him a great deal of money, and it did). The third would rule the witnesses both for and against him. The twelfth would rule the hidden motives of his secret enemy (his accuser, since he did not know who she was).

In all criminal cases, certain planetary rulerships are invariable. Saturn rules the police. Mercury rules the evidence, including alibis and fingerprints. Jupiter rules the judge.

Therefore, I used a straight horary analysis of the question: How can we get my client acquitted? And I gave him the following information while waiting for the lawyer to call him back.

First, placing his accuser in the radical seventh of open enemies, we find that the cusp is quincunx Mars, ruling the first (himself). This indicates a subtle enemy, operating under fateful compulsions, perhaps not wholly responsible for her actions. Venus, the seventh house ruler, in late Sagittarius, makes no aspect to any planet before it leaves the sign, which means her actions will not produce the result she desires. When Venus moved into Capricorn, she would be forced to change her tune.

The past history of this Venus in Sagittarius was not good. As it traversed Sagittarius it made a quincunx to Jupiter (fateful compulsion to seek notoriety, prominence); a conjunction to Mercury (talk, gossip); a square to the Moon, always an indicator of the woman in the case; the square would mean conflict with the self, between her ego represented by Venus and her emotions, the Moon; a conjunction to the South Node (fatality, disaster); a square to Saturn (failure, frustration, misbegotten notions of power); squares to Pluto and Uranus (abnormal preoccupation with sex, sexual frustration, desire to injure or attack others through sex, a longing to be raped (Pluto) and achieve sudden fame through it (Uranus); a conjunction with Mars (sexual desire, specifically for the querent whom she has accused of doing what she wanted done).

Second, considering the Moon as coruler of the woman in the case, it is also bad. The last planet it passed over was Venus, significator of the accuser. This conjunction probably marked when she identified the accused to the police as her attacker. After the Moon entered Pisces it trined Jupiter (optimism, but misplaced because Jupiter is retrograde). Then it squared Mercury (lies). It is about to square the Nodes (fatality, compulsion), and will then make a conjunction to the retrograde Saturn. In horary astrology, this movement of the Moon from Mercury to Saturn or vice versa—making bad aspects to both—is the signature of a liar or of one who bears false witness in court. It is generally read as deliberate, malicious lying, but when one or more of the planets fall in Pisces, the lying may be pathological, rooted in mental illness. This always has to be considered in a chart where there is strong emphasis on Pisces, Neptune, or the twelfth house. In some configurations like this, if the Neptune is also badly afflicted, it may indicate a poisoner as the secret enemy.

Third, the Moon rules the ninth house, which is the 3 from the seventh—the open enemy's mental condition. But this house is divided between two rulers, indicating that there were two sides to her mental processes, one subconscious (the Moon), the other visible and perhaps able to make a brilliant impression (the Sun). With the Moon so badly configured in Pisces, it seemed possible that some unresolved conflict in her subconscious mind was split off, as in schizophrenia, from conscious recognition (the Sun), and so severely repressed (Moon conjunction Saturn) that the woman had little insight into what she was doing, or why. The Sun is in a much better condition than the Moon, having just passed a trine to Saturn and applying in sextiles to Pluto and Uranus. Just after it passed the conjunction to Saturn, the Moon would trine the Sun, and I found this alarming, for it could mean that the woman would be able to create an image (the Moon) of rationality and intelligence so convincing that her lies would hold up in court and my client would be convicted. Yet the Sun did fall in her sixth house (illness), and it was parallel both the Moon and Neptune. This is a pattern indicating delusion (Neptune) afflicting and weakening the ego (the Sun).

Putting all this together, it seemed to me that Neptune in the accuser's sixth house of health just above the Ascendant, my client, was the key to a solution of the problem. He was suffering from a sneak attack by the poisoned tongue of a person who was mentally ill. The way out would be to convince his lawyer that this was the case. The lawyer would then have to convince the Court either by medical records, or, if these were unobtainable, by forcing the accuser through cross examination to reveal her unsound mind herself.

I had just finished telling my client this when the phone rang; it was the lawyer calling him back. He told her he would like her to defend him, and that he had been arrested by a vice squad detective on a charge of entering a woman's apartment through a window on the fire escape and of making lewd and obscene advances to her. This crime allegedly took place on April 14, 1965, at about 10:30 p.m.

After asking a few more questions, this lawyer, whom we will call Miss A said that the matter was indeed serious and the case interested her very much, but that she could not take it. She said that what he had told her had a familiar ring and she thought the young lady might be one who had worked in her office, whom she knew fairly well, and who claimed she had been the victim of just such an experience last April. When my client asked if this woman still worked in Miss A's office, she answered no, that the girl seemed to have a rather unstable personality, which created problems both for herself and others, and that she had left to return to school. Miss A explained that, if she took the case and the girl turned out to be the same, the fact that she had worked in Miss A's office and was well known to her would prejudice my client's case. Miss A then recommended another lawyer, a good friend of hers. The unspoken implication was that Miss A and her friend Mr. B sometimes helped each other out, behind the scenes, with pertinent information.

So far so good—a woman lawyer had proved helpful but had refused the case and referred my client to a man. And already we had testimony that the accuser was not exactly of sound mind, or at least not of sound personality. While my client tried to telephone Mr. B, I went back to the chart.

The Moon conjunct Saturn (the police) indicated that the accuser was working closely with them and was probably their only witness. She might even have established a secret (Pisces) intimate relationship with one of the cops. The police were not on sure ground, however, because Saturn was retrograde. This meant that their evidence could be shaken.

Pluto and Uranus in the radical tenth (the Court) indicated something unsavory going on there. I told my client that there was some hidden scandal (Pluto) involving the Courts that would be exposed (Uranus) very soon. I thought it would act in his favor, because Mercury in his first disposed of these planets. There is an old aphorism in horary astrology that says when the ruler of the tenth is in the first, the Court will decide in favor of the querent.

Jupiter in the radical eighth was retrograde and about to move into Gemini, which is the sign on my client's natal Ascendant. When a person (or nation) has to defend himself against an adversary action taken while Jupiter transits his natal first or tenth, his chances of victory are good. This Jupiter was in the accuser's second house of resources, and because it was retrograde, seemed to indicate that her luck would run out when it entered Gemini and turned direct. The first aspect it would make in Gemini was an opposition to Venus, ruling the accuser.

In spite of all this, I did not feel very good about the matter. There was always the possibility that my liking for this client was coloring my interpretation, and I had fallen into the trap of wishful thinking.

Mr. B took the case, for an exorbitant fee, as I had warned. (Mars at the second cusp—excessive, sudden outlay of money.) The pretrial hearing occurred at 10:00 a.m. November 5, before Judge

K. My client was confronted with his accuser, a medium tall, thin blonde of twenty-three. She and the sex squad detective were the only witnesses for the prosecution. She positively identified my client as the man who had entered her apartment through a window and made advances to her in the most obscene language, every word of which she repeated several times with relish. My client learned that she lived around the corner from him, less than a block away, but he had never seen her before to his knowledge. He also learned that he had been under police surveillance since July. It must have been the most futile waste of shoe leather in history, for during all that time he had done nothing but go to work, go to night school, call on his girl, and occasionally take her out. The surveillance hadn't been too clever, either, because he was often aware of being followed and had wondered why.

The girl was indeed the same one who had worked in Miss A's office.

My client was released on bail. The Grand Jury heard the evidence on December 6, 1965, and refused to return an indictment of felony because there was no proof that the accused had intended to commit a crime when he allegedly entered the girl's apartment. It recommended that the charge be reduced to a misdemeanor.

Then came the task for my client of trying to remember where he had been and what he had been doing on the night of April 14, and what witnesses he could get to prove it.

He had gone to night school. His teacher had recorded his attendance, still had his record book, and agreed to testify at the trial. The class let out at ten o'clock, and my client had to hurry to catch a bus home. He got a bus schedule from the transit company showing that he would have boarded the bus at 10: 05 p.m. and reached his destination at 10:20 p.m.. If he missed that bus he would have had to wait half an hour for the next one. He also got a plan of the campus showing the location of his classroom and how far he would have to walk to the bus stop. But the question was: did he always take that bus? And could he be so positive he had taken it that night?

No, he did not always take that bus. Frequently, he went after class to see his girl. How could he be sure he hadn't gone to see her that night? Because it was April 14 and he had to hurry home to do his income tax. The girl remembered that this was the reason he could not see her that night, and she agreed to testify to it at the trial.

There was still a gap of ten minutes. If he got off the bus at 10: 20 p.m., it would have taken him no more than five to get to his accuser's house. True, he would have had to sprint faster than Superman to have gone from the bus stop, climbed her fire escape, pried open the window, entered the apartment, taken off all his clothes, made obscene advances to her, and left, all before 10:30, when she called the police.

His landlady remembered, however, that he had come in shortly before 10:30 p.m., chatted with her a few minutes before going to his room to do his tax return; that he had remained in his room until well after midnight, when he had completed the return. Later, they had another short conversation, after which he went to bed. His landlady agreed to testify to this effect.

These were my client's three witnesses—all respectable, well dressed, middle-class people of a sort rarely seen in the District's Court of General Sessions.

While my client was preparing his alibi, his accuser paid frequent visits to the office of her former employer, Miss A. There, she spent many happy moments telling the office girls all the developments in the case, from her point of view. She seemed to get the greatest pleasure from talking about the ruin of my client's life and the many years he would have to spend in jail. All that she told Miss A.'s employees was immediately repeated to Mr. B. It must have given him great and helpful insight into the girl's character; but he was a very circumspect man who never repeated much of this information to my client.

All the while he was preparing his case, Mr. B tried unsuccessfully to get a copy of the original police report that must have contained the girl's first description of the incident and of her unwelcome visitor. The police had no right to withhold this, but they did, which made Mr. B quite certain it contained information detrimental to their case.

The horary chart had revealed that a scandal would come out about the courts and many of the judges, and that this would operate for my client's benefit. Suddenly, in January, the newspapers began to print stories about plea bargaining. The burden of them was that the prosecutors in the district attorney's office would persuade defendants to plead guilty by promising them short sentences. Most of these defendants were poor, ignorant of their rights, and scared to death. They had inadequate counselor none at all. Usually, they had been frightened into saying things to the police when they were arrested without having been warned that such things could be used against them. They were often defended by court-appointed lawyers who worked hand in glove with the prosecutors—lawyers who knew nothing about the case and cared less. The newspapers implied that many judges connived at this plea bargaining to clear their dockets. There were demands for the resignation or impeachment of several judges. The result of all this was that, by the time my client came to trial, every judge on the bench was most solicitous of every defendant's welfare. Each judge tried to make sure that no innocent man had been persuaded to plead guilty, that the police had warned him anything he said might be used against him, that no one in the prosecutor's office had told him what to say. To a man, the judges were bending over backward to see that every defendant got a fair trial. They had developed a very sour attitude toward the prosecutors, and they made no bones about it. For several months, the lot of a prosecutor in the D.C. courts was not a happy one.

The trial began at 2:05 p.m. on February 24, 1966. By coincidence, it came up before Judge K, who had presided at the pretrial hearing. Mr. B felt that this was advantageous. His first tactical move was flattering to the judge: he waived the defendant's privilege of a jury trial. In a horary chart, the eleventh house rules juries. In our chart, the cusp is quincunx the Moon (readjustment) and the ruler Venus is without aspect in a late degree of Sagittarius: the jury had no function and was dismissed.

The prosecution presented their first witness: the detective.

He was shaken, nervous, and on uncertain ground: Saturn (police) retrograde. Evidently, in the interval since the pretrial hearing, the possibility had dawned on him that he might have arrested the wrong man. He did not make a good impression on the Court.

The young lady was put on the stand. She positively identified my client. As the prosecutor put her through her paces she described every nuance of his obscene advances, repeating his unprintable language verbatim, even dwelling on it. She described how she had fended him off with a knife, made him pick up his clothes and leave through the window, naked as a jaybird, with his clothes in his arms. As she talked, the judge kept studying the defendant, evidently puzzled by the obvious discrepancy between his gentlemanly appearance and the actions the young lady described. She was turned over to Mr. B for cross-examination.

Mr. B: You say this man entered your second-floor apartment through a window?

Witness: Yes, sir. It was on the fire escape.

Mr. B: Was the window locked?

W: Yes.

Mr. B: You're sure of that?

W: Oh yes, positive.

Mr. B: Then this man jimmied it open?

W: I suppose so.

Mr. B: Were there marks on the frame showing this had been done?

W: I suppose so.

Mr. B: Did you see such marks?

W: I guess so. I don't remember.

Mr. B: Did you see this man enter through the window?

W: No. I was not in the room when he came in.

Mr. B: Where were you?

W: I was taking a bath.

Mr. B: Could you see him in your bedroom, perhaps through the open bathroom door?

W: No, sir. The door was closed.

Mr. B: Did you hear him moving around in the other room?

W: Not exactly. He was very sneaky and quiet. I just suddenly felt someone was there.

Mr. B: You did not hear him jimmy open the window or jump down from the sill onto the floor?

W: No. I told you, I was taking a bath.

Mr. B: Ah, yes. Please be patient with me. I'm only trying to clarify what happened in my own mind before we proceed. You were taking a bath, and suddenly you felt—you had a hunch—that someone was in your apartment. You got out of the tub and put on a robe.

W: No, sir.

Mr. B: You did not get out of the tub?

W: Yes, but I didn't wait to put on a robe.

Mr. B: Oh. You wrapped a towel around yourself.

W: No. I had no time for that.

Mr. B: You mean you got out of the tub and went into the kitchen *without anything on?* (Mr. B. was obviously, virtuously, shocked.)

W: I did not go into the kitchen. I went right into the bedroom where he was.

Mr. B: But you have testified that you drove him out with a knife. What kind of a knife was it?

W: A kitchen knife—a butcher knife.

Mr. B: Where did the knife come from?

W: (Impatiently) I had it with me in the bathroom.

Mr. B: Did it just happen to be there by chance?

W: No. I always took it into the bathroom with me, just in case.

Mr. B: In case of what?

W: In case someone should attack me when I was naked and defenseless.

Mr. B: What was this knife like? How big was it?

W: An ordinary butcher knife—about ten inches long.

Mr. B: (In tones of wonder) You *always* took a bath with a ten-inch butcher knife?

W: Yes, I did. A person can't be too careful.

Mr. B: True, true. (He turned to the judge.) Your Honor, I have not had access to the police report detailing what actually happened immediately after this young lady called them. I wonder if your Honor could ask the prosecution to let me examine this for a few moments before I proceed with my cross-examination of this witness?

The judge ordered the prosecution to give Mr. B the report and called a recess while he examined it. By this time the judge had grown visibly red in the face, but whether from suppressed laughter or fury would have been hard to say. He looked as if he could use a recess himself.

According to the report, there was no evidence that the window had been jimmied open. And the young lady had described her visitor as of medium height and build, with an orange mustache and blond hair. The defendant was clean shaven, with brown hair. He had three witnesses to testify that he had not had a mustache the previous April. While they were going over the police report, he suggested that Mr. B ask the witness if he had any hair on his chest. If she said no, he'd be willing to take off his shirt to show the Court a visible mat of black hair.

When Mr. B resumed his examination, he asked: You are absolutely sure that this is the man who entered your apartment last April 14?

W: Positive. I'd know him anywhere.

Mr. B: You couldn't possibly be mistaken? Perhaps in the excitement.

W: Absolutely not. He lives in my neighborhood, and I've often seen him in the street. I'd never forget him as long as I live.

Mr. B: Last April you told the police that he had an orange mustache. As you can see, he has no mustache at all.

W: Well, he did at that time.

Mr. B: Orange?

W: Yes.

Mr. B.: What kind of a mustache?

W.: It was just a mustache.

Mr. B: I mean, was it big and luxuriant, or a small toothbrush mustache?

W: It was ordinary, medium-sized.

Mr. B: Could you possibly have mistaken a shadow on his lip for a mustache?

W: No, I couldn't.

Mr. B: I thought perhaps the light was poor. Was it?

W: No, it wasn't. The room was brightly lighted.

Mr. B: I see. He was standing naked in a brightly lighted room. Where were his clothes?

W: He had taken them off and put them under the bed.

Mr. B: You could see his entire body clearly?

W: Yes.

Mr. B: Did he have any hair on his chest?

W: No.

Mr. B: But he did have an orange mustache?

W.: Well, it was sort of a mustache.

Mr. : What do you mean, sort of a mustache? If the light was good couldn't you tell if it was a real mustache or only a sort of mustache?

W: It looked like a mustache to me.

Mr. B: You mean it might not have looked like a mustache to someone else?

W: How do I know?

Mr. B: That's what I'm trying to determine. Now. You saw this man in a bright light, he had no hair on his chest, but he had something on his face that looked like a sort of a mustache that was medium-sized and orange, but it only looked that way to you and might not have looked that way to someone else. Is that correct?

W; No. He definitely had a sort of a mustache.

Mr. B: A sort of an orange mustache. Thank you. That will be all.

Mr. B put my client on the stand and proceeded to establish his alibi. He introduced the class attendance book as evidence. The prosecution objected, saying that it could have been cooked up at any time. Mr. B said the teacher was present and would testify that it was indeed the correct attendance book, and that the defendant had been in his class that night.

As Mr. B questioned my client, the young lady, sitting in the front row of the courtroom beside the detective, began to giggle and laugh every time the defendant spoke to answer. She whispered to the detective. As my client answered the questions, she laughed again, louder and louder. The Judge turned the color of a boiled beet with fury. He stood up and banged the bench with great, resounding whacks. He gave her a tongue lashing that would have singed the hide on a coyote. Probably no courtroom has ever been treated to a more awesome flow of judicial vituperation, delivered with such sustained fury. When he finally sat down, he asked the prosecutor, "Do you have anything more to say?"

"I guess not, your Honor."

"Do you have any more evidence?"

"No, your Honor."

"Any more *witnesses?*" The sneer in the judge's voice as he stressed the word was indescribable.

"No, your Honor."

The judge turned to my client, the defendant. "Stand up, young man."

When my client stood, the judge pounded on the bench, three times, so hard it was a wonder he didn't break his arm. "Not guilty!" he shouted. "Case dismissed!"

The time was 3: 55 p.m.

When my client thanked Mr. B, the lawyer said, "It was my pleasure—a *great* pleasure. After all, it isn't often we get a chance to defend an innocent man."

Thinking about this case, I have often wondered if there might have been any means, other than astrology, by which my client could have found the one lawyer who had employed his accuser and knew she was mentally unstable; and who had sent him to a friend so situated that he was able to capitalize on that knowledge. Such things are not coincidence. They seem like coincidence because they are hidden from common sense and common knowledge. But they are not hidden from the horoscope because there everything has something to do with the querent, and nothing can be too small to engage our attention and our respect.

21

Politics

We can sometimes make accurate political forecasts from charts cast for the moment of a significant event, such as a man's public declaration that he will run for office, the nomination of a candidate, the convening of a political convention, a Supreme Court decision, or taking an oath of office. It is easier to predict the outcome of a presidential election from horary charts erected for the moment each of the candidates was nominated than it is from their natal horoscopes or from transits over our national map.

Any astrologer who was paying close attention to the political events of 1972 could have predicted the outcome of the election from one chart alone: the nomination of Senator McGovern. Chart 19 represents this event, which occurred at 11: 57 p.m. EDT on July 12, 1972, at Miami Beach, Florida. Of course, this chart does not tell us the name of the senator's competitor or the details of the competitor's campaign. It only tells us, very clearly, that Senator McGovern would lose—no matter who ran against him. That is all you need to know to predict the outcome of an election.

In a nomination chart, the first house represents the convention, caucus, or group empowered to select a candidate. Here, 0 Aries 35 is rising, an invalid Ascendant. This means the action taken was ill-considered, premature, hasty, and would, therefore, bring a final result contrary to the one desired.

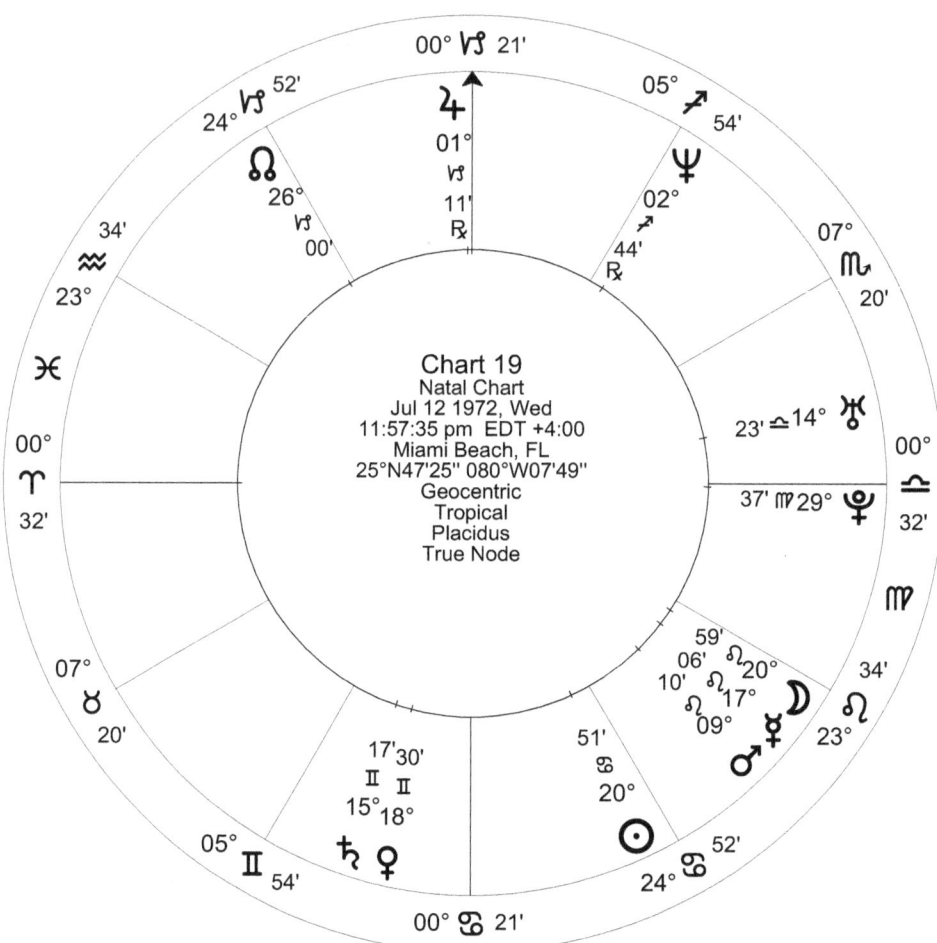

Chart 19. Event: Nomination of McGovern.
July 12, 1972, 11 h 57m 35s p.m. EDT, Miami Beach, Florida.

The seventh house rules the campaign that would be waged, and of course it has another invalid cusp: the campaign would be fruitless. Pluto (hidden machinations, strong-arm tactics, vast money interests) just under this cusp and about to leave Virgo, the sign of bureaucracy, wage earners, the proletariat, means that voters in these categories would desert the candidate during the campaign. Uranus (backlash, unexpected events, and disasters) in the seventh means much the same thing. Only one planet, Mars, can make a favorable aspect to Uranus. All the others are past it. McGovern ran on a radical (Uranus) platform designed to appeal to the proletarian voter. But Uranus here rules the twelfth house (secret enemies). During the campaign, it became public knowledge (seventh house) that the electorate regarded radicals and radical issues (Uranus) as public enemies (seventh house).

The tenth house rules the candidate—another invalid cusp.

Jupiter at the tenth of a horary chart does not necessarily presage good fortune for the person or matter involved. It depends upon the condition of retrograde Jupiter, which promised much and delivered little. Jupiter in the tenth always means notoriety, publicity, fame. Any candidate gets plenty of that. When Jupiter is retrograde and about to move back into another sign, all this is transitory, and the publicity may actually turn sour and bring results opposite to those intended.

In American political charts, Saturn rules the Democratic Party because it is the older, and Jupiter rules the Republicans. With Saturn disposing of Jupiter in this chart, great numbers of Democrats switched over in this election to vote Republican, but only for the president. Jupiter was also retrograde when Nixon was nominated, but it had gone back into Sagittarius, which rules the press. His relations with the press are bad, and they have got worse since his inauguration.

The Moon rules the electorate. Here it is void-of-course: they would not function as desired for McGovern. The Sun rules the candidate: here it is extremely weak, without vitality, because it cannot make an aspect to anything in the chart before it leaves Cancer except a conjunction to the South Node (fatality, defeat), and a sextile to Pluto.

The only close aspect in the chart is a sextile of Mercury applying to Venus. Senator McGovern has Gemini rising in his natal chart, so Mercury is his ruling planet. Probably a man needs *something* superficially favorable to get nominated to high office, even though the final result will be disaster.

There are certainly worse mundane charts than this one in existence. Maps for the onset of wars, for great natural disasters, for revolutions, and those presaging the death of kings and rulers are usually worse. But they are actively, tragically bad. They have close, heavy afflictions from malefics. This chart, with its weak Sun, its dearth of aspects, its void-of-course Moon, and invalid degrees on all the cardinal cusps is simply futile. Once the Democrats had selected a candidate at that moment—and it would not have mattered who he was—they could do nothing that would avert the worst defeat in our electoral history for their man.

The years 1972-76 mark a turning point in our political history. Other critical charts that the student might like to construct and examine are:

Nixon's nomination: August 22, 1972, 10:46 p.m., EDT, Miami Beach, Florida. The Ascendant was invalid at 1 Taurus, the Moon in Aquarius was applying to an opposition to Mercury, and Jupiter retrograde.

Agnew's nomination: August 23, 1972, 9:15 p.m. EDT, Miami Beach. Florida. Ascendant at 1 Aries 31 was invalid, Moon in Aquarius was applying to a sextile to Jupiter, and Jupiter was stationary direct.

Election: November 7, 1972, midnight, Washington, D.C. Moon void-of-course in late Scorpio. Uranus in the degree of the Nodes, and Saturn retrograde in the tenth.

Nixon's oath of office: January 20, 1973, 11:59 a.m. EST, Washington, D.C.

Vietnam War, cease-fire: January 27, 1973, 7 p.m. Washington, D.C.

Ascendant invalid at 28 Leo, Moon in late Scorpio void of course. Saturn retrograde in the tenth. Uranus stationary retrograde. The time was 8 a.m. on the following day in Hanoi, giving an invalid Ascendant at 1 Pisces 46. The retrograde Saturn in the fourth, and the stationary Uranus in the eighth. Mars in the tenth.

22

War

In mundane work, the governing chart for a war is cast for the moment when hostilities begin; that is, when the troops of one side open fire, invade, or start bombing the troops, territory or people of the other side. Years of tension and animosity may precede this, but the war itself dates from the exact moment one side takes overt, aggressive action against the other. Regardless of the causes, the moral issues involved, or which side you are on, the first house of a war chart rules the aggressor nation, the one who first commits an overt act of war. The seventh house rules the defending nation that responds to the act.

For example, in the various phases of WWII, the rulerships lined up as follows:

- The European Theatre: the first house ruled the Germans because they began the war by firing on the Polish coast from battleships.
- The Russian Theatre: the first house ruled the Germans because they invaded Russian territory.
- The Italian campaign: the first house ruled the Allies because they invaded Italy.
- The Pacific Theatre: the first house ruled the Japanese because they bombed Pearl Harbor.

The lies and propaganda that accompany wars make it difficult at times to discover which side actually fired first. In WW II, the Germans were told that the Poles began the aggressive action, and to this day they may believe it. In the Vietnam War, we were told that Hanoi's gunboats fired on our ships in the Gulf of Tonkin. Charts read from mistaken belief in false information will not yield correct results. Sincerity, morality, faith, or the virtue of your cause have nothing to do with the case. The first house rules the initiator, the seventh rules the side that responds, regardless of sympathy. If national leaders ever come to use astrology, they will probably always get the wrong answers from war charts because they always come to believe their own lies. This was Hitler's problem when he tried to benefit from astrology.

Here I will use a chart for a war long over, because its beginning was well documented and there is no doubt which side fired first. According to Beard's *Rise of American Civilization,* soldiers of South Carolina, which had seceded from the Union, fired on Fort Sumter at 4:30 a.m. on April 12, 1861. They fired against the orders of their commanding officer, but that did not matter. Their shots were the first aggressive action in the bitterest, most brutal war of our history. In the chart constructed for that moment, the first house rules the South.

A mundane horoscope of this kind is read exactly like a horary chart. The questions the nation, or the world, asks are: How will the war proceed? Which side will win? What will be the long range results when it is over? The instant a war begins, millions of people are asking those questions. Great psychic force lies behind them, and anyone able to study the chart without bias should be able to get honest answers to them.

If you do not know the exact moment hostilities began, or which side fired first, you can construct a war chart for the time and place one side declared war on the other. The map will then be read from the viewpoint of the nation making the declaration, which will be ruled by the first house. In a catastrophe like WW I, many nations were involved and they all declared war on each other at different times, in different capitals. Event charts could be set up for each of these times and places, and each chart would show the course of the war and its outcome for the nation concerned. In such charts, the seventh house would always symbolize the enemy.

I doubt that an honest analysis of a war can be obtained from a simple horary chart constructed to answer questions like: When will the war be over? Or who will win the war? Millions of people are constantly asking these questions during the entire course of the war, and they do not all have the same motivation for asking. I think the psychic confusion resulting from so many different personal involvements would result in ambiguous or invalid horary charts. Therefore, if you have no definite time and place for the construction of an exact event chart, you would probably obtain better results from using the national horoscope or that of the nation's ruler and keeping track of the transits, eclipses, and progressions as the war continues. If you combine this with similar charts for the enemy, you should be able to judge the final outcome.

Even if we have an exact event chart, we should never ignore the national chart or the ruler's, provided we have them as well. Not all attacks upon a nation result in war. Sometimes there is merely a skirmish and the matter is amicably settled. Sometimes, the event that sets the world on fire is trivial compared to the resulting holocaust. This was the case with WW I, which began when an anarchist in Sarajevo killed the Archduke Ferdinand of Austria. Europe had been spoiling for war and preparing for it for years, but several events far more serious than the assassination of an archduke did not precipitate it. Astrologically speaking, the stars were not quite right until August 1914. Then the planetary lineup was so threatening that anything, however trivial, could light the fuse. It merely happened to be an assassination.

In our own Civil War, tension between the North and the South had been building up for years. But the bloody insurrections in Kansas did not begin it, nor did John Brown's raid on Harper's Ferry. So how would we know, if we had lived in those times, whether or not the firing on Fort Sumter would provide the definitive event chart?

Mainly by comparing the event chart with the United States horoscope. In such comparisons, the Ascendant of the event chart is crucial because it is the accidental factor unique to that moment of time. If it forms an exact aspect with a natal planet *descriptive of the event*, we can assume the matter is important. If there are also exact planetary aspects between the two charts, we can assume it will have many and serious consequences.

The Ascendant for Fort Sumter is in a nearly exact square to the U.S. Mars at 20 Gemini 57. Fort Sumter Venus is within one minute of an exact opposition to the U.S. Saturn at 14 Libra 47. Fort Sumter Sun is within three minutes of an exact quincunx to the U.S. Neptune at 22 Virgo 24. In all judgments involving violence and death, the quincunx is important because it is an aspect of fatality. If there are no exact quincunxes, the judgment can be much more optimistic. There is another quincunx, which could not have been known in 1861: Pluto, ruler of Fort Sumter eighth (death), quincunx the U.S. Descendant and will retrograde back over the degree of the U.S. Nodes, in square aspect to them. Further testimony of the coming violence: the Fort Sumter Mars-Uranus conjunction straddles the U.S. Ascendant and Uranus. The U.S. Neptune is conjunct the Fort Sumter Descendant.

From all this, we could conclude that the event was extremely serious and would result in a long and bloody war, and that communication and mutual understanding between the two sides would suffer serious rupture (a fatal break) because Fort Sumter MC is less than one minute from an exact quincunx to U.S. Mercury at 24 Cancer 28. Mercury is coruler with Uranus of the U.S. horoscope.

Another indication of long-lasting failure of communication and understanding between the two sides is that Fort Sumter Jupiter rules the ninth house of the event chart (ideals, law, and philosophy) and it also rules the tenth (honor). It is retrograde, indicating that for the South, ideals, law, philosophy, and honor were committed to an archaic system of values that had long since become impractical and ruinously expensive; no matter who won the war, the values revolving

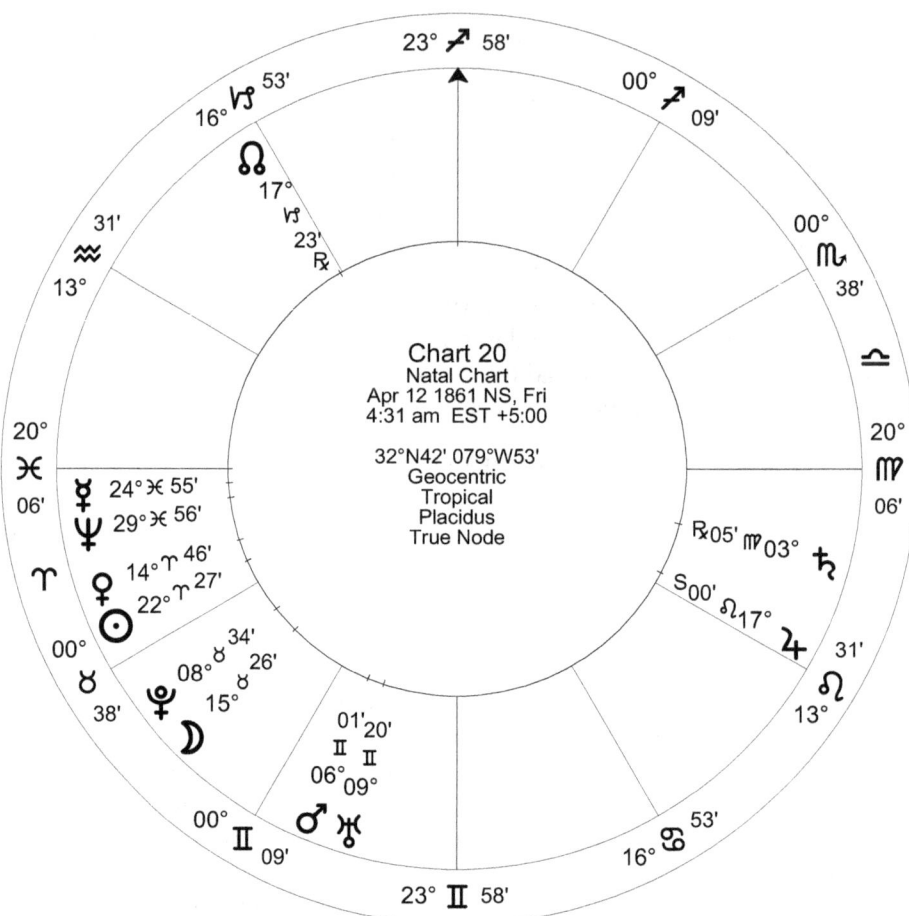

Chart 20. Event: The firing on Fort Sumter.
April 12, 1861, 4:30 a.m. Lat. 32N42, Long. 79W53.

around slavery would have to go. Another indication of the coming demise of such values is the position of Fort Sumter Jupiter quincunx the North Node. This Jupiter is also approaching an opposition to the U.S. Moon (American people) and will again make the opposition after turning direct. Thus, the action at Fort Sumter set the seal of fatality upon the institution of slavery and divided the people (opposition) into two warring factions over concepts of law, philosophy, morality, and honor.

To judge which side would win, we would use the event chart alone. The first house rules the Confederacy because secession troops initiated the action by firing on Fort Sumter. Therefore, the seventh house rules the Union. The two rulers of the seventh are Mercury and Venus, both placed in the first house (Confederacy). When your enemy occupies your own territory, you can

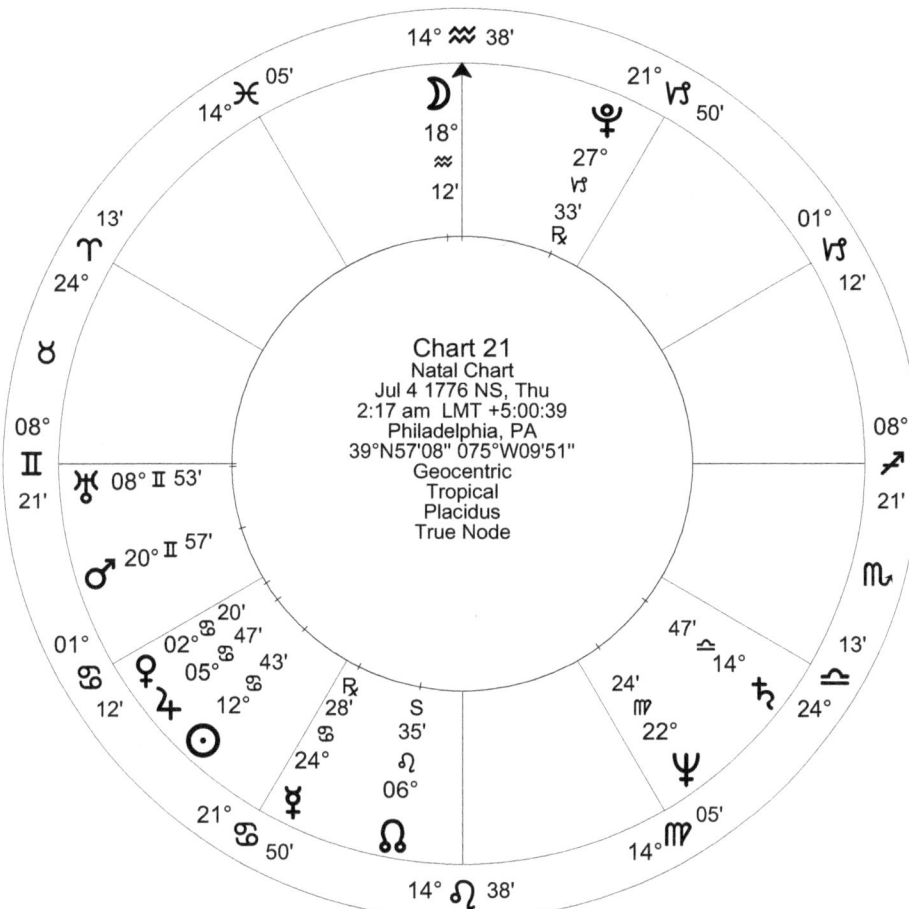

Chart 21. The horoscope of the United States of America.
July 4, 1776, 2:17 a.m. Philadelphia, Pennsylvania.

be sure of grievous troubles and perhaps ultimate defeat. The chances of a Confederate defeat are greatly increased by the trine of one of these rulers (Venus) to the retrograde Jupiter in the Confederate sixth house (armed forces). This trine would have the effect of euphorious optimism in the South, and (Jupiter retrograde) a tremendous initial push against the Union. For the first half of the war, the South won all the battles, which greatly increased their optimism.

Another interesting feature of this aspect is that Libra, the sign of strategy, rules generals. Practically all the generals and high-level officers in the U.S. Army were Southerners and went over to the Confederate cause. General Lee, one of the greatest this or any country ever produced, is personally symbolized by this Jupiter. Apparently, he knew that he could not win, yet his sense of honor (tenth) forced his allegiance to the Southern cause.

He may have known what is indicated by the retrograde Saturn in the South's sixth house of armies, in Virgo, the sign of supplies and *cotton*. Eventually, after a glorious beginning, the attrition of Saturn would take over. His armies would grow more tattered and hungry as the Northern blockade (Saturn) prevented the export of cotton, the South's principal source of wealth.

The Northern armies are ruled by the twelfth house (sixth from the seventh). With the idealism of Aquarius, most Northern soldiers went off to the slaughter convinced that they were fighting to right a horrible wrong and free the slaves. However, Uranus, ruling this house, is conjunction Mars in Gemini, a sign that tends to improvise with gimmicks. The Northern generals, who were almost all civilians with no knowledge of strategy, were certainly gimmicks. Grant, who was finally put in charge of the Union forces, had resigned from the Regular Army under a cloud. He was an outcast (Uranus), and only by a series of the most unexpected and lucky Uranian circumstances was he *accidentally* (Uranus) brought forward and called to Lincoln's attention.

The pincer movement Grant devised, which finally won the war, is described by this Mars-Uranus conjunction in Gemini, the sign which symbolizes splitting, division (the pincer movement) and also symbolizes two acting in cooperation. After sealing off the Mississippi at Vicksburg, Grant took charge of the Army of the Potomac to confront Lee. Sherman (Mars), in command of the Army of the Tennessee, cut the South in half in his march from Shiloh to the sea, burning and destroying everything in his path. Notice 24 Gemini 30 on the fourth-house cusp, representing the land and homes of the South, in a close square to Mercury, ruler of the fourth house, in another double-bodied sign. Could there be a better description of the house divided against itself?

Grant's strategy made the Civil War a textbook case, studied by subsequent generals as a model. This was the strategy the Germans used in the Franco-Prussian War, World War I and World War II. But the consequences of the first shot fired at Fort Sumter were even more far-reaching. This was actually the first modern war, where many innovations now taken for granted were used for the first time. Railroads were first used then to move troops and supplies, and cutting the rail communications of the South was a major tactical objective of Sherman's march to the sea. It saw the first use of aerial observation, from balloons; the first use of the telegraph in war, of iron clad ships, of female nurses, of cartridges and of rifled gun barrels. It was the first total war in the sense that devastation of the civilian economy was deliberately planned and carried out because, for the first time, the military perceived civilian labor and wealth as an enemy asset. Probably, it was also the first to set up the ghastly prisoner of war camps, which were a disgrace to both sides. The old view, that war was a gentleman's game, had begun to crumble during Napoleon's campaigns, but even then prisoners were usually shot, quickly exchanged, or left to find their way back to their own lines. Prisoners were felt to be an intolerable burden. During the Civil War the modern attitude was born, namely, that the best enemy soldier was a dead one; next best was a prisoner.

It is difficult to find and evaluate innovations in an event chart because it is the nature of radical inventions to remain unknown until they are used. But the three outer planets are closely involved with modern technology, and when one of them rises or is close to the MC we can suspect that innovations of some sort will be important. Here, the rising Neptune conjunction Mercury may explain much of this inspired wickedness. Neptune rules hospitals and nurses, balloons, ships, and POW camps. Other things first used in war (Mars) are ruled by Uranus: railroads, telegraph, and the new type guns.

The immediate cause of the war, as both sides saw it, was slavery: Mercury conjunction Neptune, symbol of both the Negro race and of slaves, in Pisces, the sign of bondage. But Neptune is only three minutes from 0 Aries, a sign of freedom. This is a clear indication that the slaves would be freed, no matter what else happened.

The final outcome for the Confederacy is shown by the fourth house with its cusp square its ruler, Mercury, which is also the ruler of the Union. The Mercury-Neptune conjunction in Pisces shows that the South was romantically deceived about its powers. The final outcome would be defeat and bankruptcy (Neptune). The fourth house for the South is the tenth for the North. The horrors of the reconstruction, the deliberate looting of the South by the carpetbaggers, the suspension of Civil Rights for white Southerners, and the vindictive malice of the conquerors are all shown by this conjunction in the Ascendant of the Confederacy. Neptune gone wrong does lasting harm of a very subtle nature: it undermines the foundations and encourages decay. The effects of this are still with us.

In judgments like this, it is important to remember that, unlike Mars and Saturn, which can also be very cruel, Neptune is never just.

The outcome for the North is shown by the tenth (fourth from the seventh). Ruled by a retrograde Jupiter, victory was slow in coming and the cost of it was untold damage to the whole country. But it *was* victory because Venus, coruler of the Union, occupies the enemy's Ascendant and is trine Jupiter. Remember: a retrograde Jupiter denies an expansion of power to the side which fires first.

An interesting detail of this chart is the fate of both presidents, symbolized by the Sun, which is in an exact quincunx to the U.S. Neptune. Both leaders suffered a different kind of fatality (quincunx). Jefferson Davis was tried and convicted of treason (Neptune). Lincoln was shot by a madman (Neptune).

If you had been alive in 1861 and had set up this horoscope on the morning after the event, what would you, or could you, have done to turn all this destructive mass Karma into more constructive channels? A good astrologer (except for the knowledge of Pluto) could have read most of this in the chart. Good astrologers do this sort of thing at least several times a month, so it's not merely a matter of hindsight.

Use your own natal chart to decide. After all, if you'd been born in those times, your chart would have been different but it would have been descriptive of much the same person you are today. Through all our lives, we are always the same people, no matter when we are born. We merely do different things with our lives at different times.

www.ingramcontent.com/pod-product-compliance
Lightning Source LLC
Chambersburg PA
CBHW081838170426
43199CB00017B/2771